Institute for Research on Public Policy

Institut de recherche en politiques publiques

FOUNDED IN 1972, THE INSTITUTE FOR RESEARCH ON Public Policy is an independent, national, nonprofit organization.

IRPP seeks to improve public policy in Canada by generating research, providing insight and sparking debate that will contribute to the public policy decision-making process and strengthen the quality of the public policy decisions made by Canadian governments, citizens, institutions and organizations.

IRPP's independence is assured by an endowment fund, to which federal and provincial governments and the private sector have contributed.

The Canadian Institute for Research on Regional Development, located on the campus of the Université de Moncton, was established in 1983. It is an independent, nonprofit organization governed by a board of directors. Through its research, publication and conferences programs, it seeks to encourage continuing research into questions relating to regional development.

The Institute views the study of regional development from a broad perspective and encourages a multidisciplinary approach including economics, economic geography, political science, public policy and sociology.

The institute's goals are twofold:

1. To act as a catalyst in promoting informed public debate on regional development issues.
2. To make available to all interested parties objective information and data pertaining to the study of regional development.

Scholars with an interest in undertaking research on regional development issues are invited to contact the institute. Our Web site is: www.umoncton.ca/icrdr

FONDÉ EN 1972, L'INSTITUT DE RECHERCHE EN politiques publiques (IRPP) est un organisme canadien, indépendant et sans but lucratif.

L'IRPP cherche à améliorer les politiques publiques canadiennes en encourageant la recherche, en mettant de l'avant de nouvelles perspectives et en suscitant des débats qui contribueront au processus décisionnel en matière de politiques publiques et qui rehausseront la qualité des décisions que prennent les gouvernements, les citoyens, les institutions et les organismes canadiens.

L'indépendance de l'IRPP est assurée par un fonds de dotation, auquel ont souscrit le gouvernement fédéral, les gouvernements provinciaux et le secteur privé.

IRPP

Institute for Research on Public Policy

Institut de recherche en politiques publiques

L'Institut canadien de recherche sur le développement régional a été créé en 1983 et est établi sur le campus de l'Université de Moncton. Organisme indépendant et sans but lucratif, il est régi par un conseil d'administration. Son mandat est de promouvoir la recherche sur les questions relatives au développement régional dans le cadre notamment de programmes de recherche, de publication et de conférences.

L'Institut envisage l'étude du développement régional dans une perspective très large et souhaite favoriser une approche pluridisciplinaire, incluant l'économie, la géographie économique, la science politique, les politiques publiques et la sociologie.

Les objectifs de l'Institut sont les suivants :

1. susciter un débat public éclairé sur le développement régional;
2. rendre accessibles des informations et des données objectives à ce sujet.

Tout spécialiste intéressé à entreprendre des recherches sur les questions de développement régional est invité à communiquer avec l'Institut. Son site Internet est à l'adresse suivante : www.umoncton.ca/icrdr

The Art of the State II

Thinking North America

Thomas J. Courchene,

Donald J. Savoie and

Daniel Schwanen, editors

Printed in Canada
Dépôt légal 2004

National Library of Canada
Bibliothèque nationale du Québec

CANADIAN CATALOGUING IN PUBLICATION DATA

Thinking North America / editors, Thomas J. Courchene, Donald J. Savoie and Daniel Schwanen.

(Art of the state; v. 2)
To be complete in 8 folios.
Proceedings of a conference held Oct. 17-18, 2003, Montebello, Quebec. Contents: Folio 2. A new accommodation with the United States: the trade and economic dimension / Michael Hart — folio 3. The role of sub-national governments in North American integration / Earl H. Fry.
ISBN 0-88645-212-0 (set of 8 folios)

1. North America—Congresses. 2. Free trade—North America—Congresses. 3. North America—Economic integration—Congresses. 4. Subnational governments—North America—Congresses. I. Courchene, Thomas J., 1940- II. Savoie, Donald J., 1947- III. Schwanen, Daniel, 1959- IV. Institute for Research on Public Policy V. Series: Art of the state (Montréal, Quebec); v. 2.

E38.T44 2004 970 C2004-901775-6

PROJECT DIRECTORS
Thomas J. Courchene
Donald J. Savoie
Daniel Schwanen

COPY EDITOR
Marilyn Banting

PROOFREADING
Francesca Worrall

COVER AND INTERIOR DESIGN
Schumacher Design

COVER ILLUSTRATION
Normand Cousineau

INTERIOR PRODUCTION
Chantal Létourneau

PUBLISHED BY
The Institute for Research on Public Policy (IRPP)
l'Institut de recherche en politiques publiques
1470 Peel Street, Suite 200
Montreal, Quebec H3A 1T1
Tel: 514-985-2461
Fax: 514-985-2559
E-mail: irpp@irpp.org
www.irpp.org

To cite this document:

Hart, Michael. 2004. "A New Accommodation with the United States: The Trade and Economic Dimension." No. 2 of *Thinking North America*, edited by Thomas J. Courchene, Donald J. Savoie, and Daniel Schwanen. *The Art of the State*, vol. 2. Montreal: Institute for Research on Public Policy.

THIS YEAR MARKS THE 15TH ANNIVERSARY OF THE CANADA-US FREE TRADE Agreement (FTA) and the 10th anniversary of the North American Free Trade Agreement (NAFTA) coming into force. While these anniversaries would rather naturally have led to increased interest in ways to broaden and deepen our North American trading relationships, the tragic events of 9/11 have added homeland security as a complicating issue to the already full free trade agenda. With this in mind, in October 2003 the IRPP convened its second "Art of the State" conference around the theme "Thinking North America: Prospects and Pathways." Outstanding experts from Canada, Mexico and the United States came together to explore new ideas, new instruments and new processes for enriching our North American experience in ways that at the same time preserve Canada's freedom to manoeuver. We attempted to remedy gaps in the public discourse and understanding of how three proud and sovereign nations could advance common causes and manage their increasing interdependence. In this context, it is a pleasure to acknowledge our partner in this endeavour, the Canadian Institute for Research on Regional Development at the University of Moncton.

The concrete result of this conference is the series of papers of which this folio is an integral part. The contributions will be released individually, but together form a collection that will explore a wide range of North American issues, including:

- The trade and economic dimensions of the Canada-US relationship
- The pros and cons of an enhanced institutional structure, including the possibility of a treaty for a revitalized community of North Americans
- The deep determinants of integration; whether a North American "citizenship" can evolve from current relationships; and whether new rights should be extended to private parties to give direct effect to commitments by governments
- The management of environmental issues
- The role of states and provinces in any future trilateral relationship
- How efforts at making North American integration work better should be seen in light of other international agendas being pursued by the three nations, in particular that of the Free Trade Area of the Americas

On behalf of the IRPP, I want to express my sincerest thanks to the many contributors to these volumes and to extend my appreciation of their efforts to develop their ideas to new levels of depth, clarity and relevance to policy. This is due in no small part to the diligence of the three co-chairs of the second "Art of the State" conference and editors of this collection: IRPP Senior Scholar Thomas Courchene, Senior Fellow Donald Savoie and Senior Economist Daniel Schwanen. It is their hope and mine that this series will be useful to all those involved in the multifaceted North American relationships and that, mindful of potential pitfalls ahead, this work will also help train our eyes on the rewards that the three nations could reap from improving those relationships.

Hugh Segal
Montreal, March 15, 2004

A New Accommodation with the United States: The Trade and Economic Dimension

In the settlement of differences between the United States and Canada, we have the inestimable advantage of speaking (for the most part) the same language, and that not merely in the linguistic sense, for we have, in larger measure than is the case in Continental Europe, the same values, the same standards, in part the same traditions.

Prime Minister Mackenzie King, at the Imperial Conference, 1923

Canada, I have long believed, is fighting a rearguard action against the inevitable...Sooner or later commercial imperatives will bring about free movement of all goods back and forth across our long border; and when that occurs, or even before it does, it will become unmistakably clear that countries with economies so inextricably intertwined must also have free movement of the other vital factors of production — capital, services and labor.

George W. Ball, US Undersecretary of State, 1962-63

There is no worse prescription for Canadian foreign policy [than trying to differentiate ourselves from the United States]. The potential for influencing the world's greatest power is what gives us credibility in other capitals. It's our comparative advantage. As US power grows, so does Canada's opportunity...If Canadians do indeed want to make a difference, we must return to the basics of our earlier reputation in world affairs. The quality of our diplomacy, the pragmatism, flexibility and vision of our leaders, the firm commitment to principles and values, the willingness to commit significant human, material and financial resources — these are the necessary ingredients for refashioning a foreign policy of which Canadians can again be proud.

Allan Gotlieb, former Canadian ambassador to the United States, 2003

In a paper published in 2003 by the C.D. Howe Institute, Bill Dymond and I conclude that political, economic, security and other factors point to a growing need for Canada and the United States to reach a new accommodation to govern the accelerating integration of their two societies.[1] Such an accommodation needs to be considered from a variety of perspectives. This paper, however, is limited to the trade and economic dimensions, but accepts that other dimensions, from defence and security to foreign policy and immigration, all need to be considered and discussed before Canadians and Americans alike will be ready to take decisions. This paper argues that:

- The Canadian and American economies have become much more intertwined over the past 20 years in response to demands by Canadians and Americans for each other's products, services, capital and ideas, creating jobs and wealth across many sectors and accelerating the forces of mutually beneficial integration.
- The framework of rules and institutions developed over the past 70 years have worked well to facilitate and govern this process of "silent," market-led integration, but the continued presence of a heavily administered border and of similar but differentiated regulatory regimes continues to undermine the ability of both firms and individuals to reap the full benefits of deepening integration.
- The continued presence of the border poses a threat to the integrity of cross-border supply chains, particularly in a world that has become more sensitive to security threats, while the development of a less intrusive border built on enhanced trust and mutual confidence will amplify opportunities to invest in a seamless North American economy.
- A new, deep-integration agreement needs to be an integral part of a larger and more ambitious project to design ways that the two governments can work together to govern their common economic space to the mutual benefit of their citizens. Such a bilateral accommodation needs to engage the full spectrum of issues where the two societies connect and have common interests, from security and immigration to the regulation of consumer safety and the treatment of third-country goods. In each instance, the case for co-operation is well established by years of informal practice, but it now needs to be reinforced and upgraded by more formal arrangements.
- The key to a successful agreement will be the establishment of flexible institutions capable of addressing the dynamic nature of modern markets and regulatory regimes. Markets work best when reinforced by limber but effective institutions, including co-operative bilateral institutions.

- In the absence of an active approach to building institutions and procedures for joint governance, Canada faces one of two undesirable prospects: either to drift toward US-determined default positions on most matters related to the regulation of the market or to make a conscious effort to assert Canadian regulatory independence. In both instances, Canada will enjoy the illusion of independence and the reality of economic performance well below potential.
- Canada and the United States initially need to approach this challenge on a bilateral basis, but without prejudice to eventually extend similar provisions to Mexico as part of a trilateral accommodation.

To reach these conclusions, this paper examines the extent of bilateral integration and the issues it raises, the political and policy context within which such issues need to be addressed, and the contours of what might be involved in developing a modern, post-NAFTA (North American Free Trade Agreement) arrangement for the governance of the integrated Canada-US economy. It proceeds from a Canadian perspective and is primarily addressed to a Canadian audience. The paper begins with a brief review of the national mood and the range of opinions and ideas currently competing for attention.

The National Mood

In a blistering critique of Canadian foreign policy delivered as the C.D. Howe Institute's 2003 Benefactors Lecture, historian Jack Granatstein concluded that "the endemic anti-Americanism in Canada, a product of history, proximity and a different institutional culture, does Canada no credit. This attitude will not change, however, without leadership from the same political and cultural elites who regrettably continue to use anti-Americanism for their own purposes. It should be obvious to everyone that anti-Americanism hurts, rather than helps, Canada in dealing with the superpower with which it shares the continent" (Granatstein 2003, 4). He has a point, but polling suggests that political and cultural elites may have less influence than is often assumed.

Polling done over the course of the past few years indicates the extent to which Canadians have come to terms with bilateral trade liberalization and closer Canada-US trade and economic ties. In a March 1999 Ekos poll, for example, most respondents generally felt either indifferent (25 percent) or positive and optimistic (52 percent) about globalization, and similarly about trade liberalization (70 percent or more described themselves as either indifferent or optimistic and confident that liberalization will be rewarding for Canada). Nearly half of those polled believed that trade has contributed to Canadian technology development and innovation and has increased jobs, with fewer than a quarter expressing concerns about the impact of trade on cultural identity. Canadians continued to believe, however, that the government should not allow trade agreements to compromise social and environmental programs. Cultural and national identity issues were no longer serious preoccupations (Ekos 2000).

An Ekos poll taken in the spring of 2001 indicated that while 58 percent of Canadians did not foresee Canada joining the United States in the future, only 22 percent did not anticipate the evolution of deeper North American economic integration over the same time period (*National Post*, 4 June 2001).[2]

Polling in August 2001 continued to confirm this assessment. Liberal pollster Michael Marzolini found that 85 percent of Canadians supported closer trade and economic ties with the United States and 75 percent would even support closer social and cultural connections. He cautioned, however, that Canadians continue to be allergic to such words as "integration" and "harmonization" (*Ottawa Citizen*, 24 August 2001). These findings were confirmed by a smaller *National Post*/COMPAS poll which found that 64 percent of Canadians want to see a freer flow of goods and services across the border (*National Post*, 25 August 2001).

Polling soon after 11 September 2001 (9/11) indicated that an impressive 85 percent of Canadians wanted the government to adopt "much tougher" immigration and refugee laws and 76 percent believed Canada should harmonize its anti-terrorism laws with those of the United States as quickly as possible. Results from the polls suggest an increasing level of comfort with the noncommercial aspects of deepening integration (*National Post*, 29 September 2001).

While this level of support for Canada-US cross-border co-operation on non-economic measures may have weakened in subsequent months as the intensity of feelings generated by the events of 9/11 faded, polling continued to show high levels of support for closer ties with the United States across a wide range of issues. Marzolini, for example, continues to find strong support for closer ties to the United States. In a March 2003 poll, he found that an astonishing 90 percent of Canadians favoured closer economic ties and two out of three Canadians even supported closer social and cultural ties. Marzolini notes that "these results are consistent with what we've seen over the past couple of years...Canadians are interested in making the most of our close proximity to the United States" (Weber 2003). Canadians also show a growing awareness of the impact of border security measures on bilateral trade and investment interests. An Ipsos-Reid October 2003 poll found that 63 percent of Canadians believe that enhanced border security measures hinder bilateral trade, while 33 percent believe it is helpful.

A June 2003 Ipsos-Reid poll indicated that 70 percent of Canadians support NAFTA, even though only 51 percent believe it benefited Canada. The *Globe and Mail*'s Ottawa bureau chief Shawn McCarthy concludes that "the poll suggests that Canadians are mostly content with the agreement and see closer integration in the North American economy as a positive trend for Canada." Liberals were among the most supportive at 77 percent, followed by Conservatives at 75 percent, but even among New Democrats only 39 percent said NAFTA had hurt Canada. Four out of five young people said they supported closer economic integration (McCarthy 2003b).

At the same time, Canadians indicate a much higher ambivalence about US foreign policy, the war in Iraq and US flexing of its hyperpower muscles. Much of this ambivalence translates into a dislike of President George W. Bush and the current Republican administration. A summer 2003 Environics poll indicated that three out of five Canadians have an unfavourable opinion of Bush, making him the most unpopular president among Canadians in 20 years (McCarthy 2003a). The war's impact on Canadian attitudes toward closer ties with the United States, however, appears minimal. A March 2003 survey by the Centre for Research and Information in Canada (CRIC) found that only one in four Canadians want the government to put more distance between Canada and the United States (2003). That Canadians' comfort level with the United States goes beyond trade and economic interests was confirmed by an SES/Sun Media poll in May 2003. Three out of five Canadians support Canada's participation in the US missile defence shield, despite high levels of critical commentary from Canadian elites.[3]

This new level of comfort is broadly shared geographically and conceptually — across the country and across a wide range of issues — with the distinct exception of policy and media elites. Canada's political and media elites, for whom freer trade in general and closer economic ties with the United States in particular still conjure up negative images, appear to be out of touch with the mood in the country, as was the case in the early 1980s when polling indicated similarly high, if perhaps uninformed, levels of support for freer trade with the United States. Sustained opposition by economic and cultural nationalists gradually reduced this support to a bare plurality, while the pain of post-CUFTA (Canada-US Free Trade Agreement) adjustment (deepened by the Bank of Canada's attack on inflation) reduced support even further. The combined effect of CUFTA's positive longer-term economic impact and of the extent to which the anxieties of the 1988 electoral campaign proved unwarranted restored support both for freer trade and for good Canada-US trade and economic relations to historically more normal levels.

The excesses of the 1988 campaign also made Canadians wary of grandiose claims by either proponents or opponents of trade agreements. Over the past decade, Canadians have become much more pragmatic in their assessments of such initiatives. The *Globe and Mail*'s editor, Edward Greenspon, concludes:

> Twenty-first-century Canadians are not the same people as twentieth-century Canadians. They are far more pragmatic, and therefore less ideological. They are more demanding and less trusting...As the 1990s progressed, suspicions about free trade gave way to a widespread view that not only was a continental economy inevitable, but that it delivered opportunity as well as risk...The message, in essence, is this: "We're willing to grow closer economically if that's what it takes to ensure prosperity. But don't ask us to give up those things that truly give us meaning as a people. We want your best and our best."[4] (Greenspon 2001, F4)

In sum, the national mood suggests that Canadians are receptive to bilateral initiatives that can be shown to benefit Canadian trade and economic interests, but that building and maintaining support for any such initiative will require leadership.[5] Latent anti-American sentiment may not have disappeared from Canadians' attitudes, but its more corrosive aspects seem to be held by a diminishing minority. In recognition of this changing mood, growing awareness of the negative impact of deteriorating relations over the past three or four years, and broad acceptance that deepening integration has raised new challenges, Canadian analysts have, in the words of *Maclean's* columnist Mary Janigan, "churned out a breathtaking number of integration proposals" (2003).

Competing Views

Renewed interest in addressing Canada-US trade issues through a new round of negotiations first began to emerge in the period leading up to the tenth anniversary of the negotiation and implementation of the Canada-US Free Trade Agreement. At two conferences sponsored by Michigan State University in September 1998 (Kreinin 2000) and McGill University in June 1999 (MacDonald 2000), for example, former ministers and negotiators, as well as policy analysts, considered the economic and political impacts of CUFTA and discussed prospects for pursuing the "unfinished" agenda. Similarly, at a workshop organized by the Centre for Trade Policy and Law in December 1999, a group of 25 government and nongovernment specialists considered the prospect of negotiations to address the unfinished agenda.[6] Concurrently, analysts in the Micro-economic Policy Analysis Branch of the Department of Industry were hard at work pursuing a major research initiative aimed at providing a firmer intellectual and statistical basis for understanding the extent and implications of bilateral linkages in a rapidly integrating North America (see Harris 2003; St. Jacques 2003).

Interesting as this work may have been to economic and policy analysts, it failed to capture much attention among policy-makers. Lip service might occasionally be paid to the evolving Canada-US or trilateral agenda, but it failed to capture priority attention among senior officials or their political masters. Officials charged with the management of Canada-US relations, of course, broadly shared the view that a new round of negotiations to address unfinished business, as well as emerging newer issues, would be helpful, but they also appreciated that such negotiations were not likely to occur in the immediate future. Officials engaged in managing increasing congestion at the border, flowing from the surge in bilateral trade, succeeded in gaining authority to explore a range of new bilateral, co-operative efforts, as well as the resources and authority to implement various programs to ease congestion, from new infrastructure investments to better use of technology.[7] The experience of officials engaged in these efforts often found higher levels of enthusiasm on the Canadian side of the border. Similarly, Trade and Foreign Affairs officials with broad trade and investment mandates found that officials with regulatory responsibilities were less quick to see the wisdom of reducing the impact of border congestion than they themselves were. Both co-operative and unilateral initiatives, therefore, were confined to what could be pursued within existing legislative frameworks.

This state of affairs changed abruptly and dramatically in the period immediately following the terrorist attack of 9/11. The impact of this attack on US attitudes toward the outside world, including its border with Canada, had a galvanizing effect on policy discussions. The virtual closure of the border in the days immediately after 9/11 concentrated minds. Business groups, for example, previously lukewarm about the Canada-US trade policy agenda, called for immediate action by the federal government to address this new threat to the security of their access to the US market;[8] newspaper pundits expressed increasing concern with this threat to Canada's long-term prosperity (see, e.g., Fagan 2002; Sears 2002); and policy entrepreneurs found newly receptive audiences.[9]

Bill Dymond and I were among the first to publish a paper outlining the need to refine the trade and economic agenda in light of the security reality ushered in by the increased terrorist threat. In *Common Borders, Shared Destinies*, we provided a detailed outline of the emerging trade and security agenda (Dymond and Hart 2001b). Since then, a growing number of papers, speeches, workshops, conferences and opinion pieces have dissected Canada-US trade, economic and security issues from every conceivable angle and proposed a range of solutions. People and organizations participating in the debate are numerous and varied.

Former Canadian ambassador to the United States, Allan Gotlieb, who has been among the most vocal and visionary, has suggested that Canada and the United States establish a joint community of law to foster joint rules, procedures, and institutions to govern common interests in creating a more open and more secure Canada-United States economic space (Gotlieb 2003c).

His successor, Derek Burney, has called for the two governments to work together on an initiative that addresses US concerns on the security front and Canadian priorities on trade and investment matters; like Gotlieb, he is convinced that only a major initiative has the scope to attract US political interest and provide room for mutually beneficial trade-offs (Burney 2003, 2004).

The Bank of Canada governor, David Dodge (2003) has challenged the two governments to pay serious attention to the benefits of deeper integration, including a more open and integrated labour market, allowing Canadians and Americans to work wherever opportunity beckons.

The Canadian Council of Chief Executives has adopted a strategy put forward by its president and chief executive officer, Thomas d'Aquino, that focuses on five main areas for action: reinventing borders, maximizing economic efficiencies, negotiating a comprehensive resource security pact, sharing in continental and global security, and developing twenty-first century institutions to manage the new partnership. The strategy forms the basis of the Council's North American Security and Prosperity Initiative.[10]

The C.D. Howe Institute, under the leadership of University of Toronto business economist Wendy Dobson, has commissioned a series of "Border Papers" series aimed at creating a better intellectual foundation for consideration of a joint Canada-US strategy that is big enough to attract US political attention and to address the full gamut of economic and security issues now affecting bilateral relations. The series includes work from both Canadian and American analysts; some 12 papers have now been published, examining everything from the prospects for a customs union to the impact of enhanced security on bilateral trade flows (Dobson 2002; also Goldfarb 2003).

Institute for Research on Public Policy (IRPP) president, Hugh Segal, in a series of speeches over the past few years, has similarly challenged Canadians to think big and creatively about Canada-US relations with a view to developing new rules and institutions to govern joint interests.

IRPP analyst Daniel Schwanen has written various articles examining the pros and cons of further governance arrangements to foster deeper integration, arguing that the need to proceed is clear, but he cautions that security and market access arrangements should be pursued on their own merits and not used as trade-offs in a "grand bargain"; he is currently at work on drafting the contours of a "Treaty of North America" that will address the access-security nexus (Schwanen 2001, 2003).

Tom Courchene of the School of Policy Studies, Queen's University, and also IRPP Senior Scholar, directed his presidential address to the North American Economics and Finance Association to alternative approaches to broadening the deepening North American integration (Courchene 2003).

Fraser Institute analysts, particularly Fred McMahon and Martin Collacott, have been building a case for more active efforts to link trade and economic and security interests with a view to creating both more open and more secure cross-border ties.[11]

The Conference Board of Canada (2002), on the other hand, has argued that Canada needs to approach the bilateral agenda incrementally, solving problems where it can and avoiding linkages to the extent possible. At the same time, in its *Performance and Potential 2002-2003* report, the Board called for a Canadian debate on various options for securing access to the US market, up to and including a North American customs union (Barrett and Williams 2003; Barry 2003).

The Public Policy Forum held a number of consultations and sponsored research aimed at determining business attitudes toward the evolving Canada-US trade and economic agenda, much of which points to the need for a new round of bilateral discussions.[12]

University of Alberta business economist Rolf Mirus (2001) has circulated various papers suggesting that Canada-US economic integration has reached the stage at which a customs union or common market arrangement is required to capture the full benefits of integration.

McGill legal scholar Armand de Mestral (2003) advocates that Canada and the United States move toward upgrading the legal commitments in the NAFTA from intergovernmental treaty commitments to rights and obligations that have a "direct effect," allowing citizens to pursue rights under the agreement through the domestic courts, analogous to the direct effect that is central to the implementation of the treaties establishing the European Union (de Mestral 2003).

Economists Tom Courchene and Richard Harris initiated a lively debate a few years ago when they made the case for a common currency to advance Canadian macroeconomic and trade and investment interests (Courchene and Harris 1999; Courchene 2003).

Queen's political scientist Bob Wolfe insists that the need for action has been exaggerated: most issues are already well in hand or can be addressed within the framework of existing rules and institutions (Wolfe 2003).

Nationalist critics, from Stephen Clarkson to Peter Newman, have raised their voices, warning that any new initiative with the United States would threaten Canadian sovereignty and undermine Canada's ability to chart its own course (Clarkson 2002; Newman 2003).[13]

Economist Andrew Jackson (2003) believes that pursuit of the "big idea" threatens the expression of distinctive Canadian values on defence, international affairs and immigration and refugee issues. It limits Canada's necessary ability to shape industrial development, control the energy sector, move toward a more environmentally sustainable economy, levy taxes at the level needed to maintain a distinctive Canadian social model and limit the impacts of international trade and investment agreements.[14]

His colleague at the Centre for Policy Alternatives, Bruce Campbell (2003), has proposed as an alternative to the deep integration approach, "the deliberate pursuit of small steps" (2003), a strategy whose cumulative effect may over time be a government prepared to challenge NAFTA in key areas where national interests take precedence.[15]

Journalist Murray Dobbin wants to slow down the free trade "juggernaut" by radically restructuring the Department of Foreign Affairs and International Trade (DFAIT) to ensure that social, cultural, environmental and domestic economic policy goals and objectives are given primary status in Canada's trade and investment negotiations with other countries (Dobbin 2003).[16]

A few US analysts have also begun to consider the issues and examine them through the lens of US perceptions and interests. American University scholar Robert Pastor has for a number of years worked to make the case for a much more robust set of institutions and obligations to knit all three countries of North America into a tighter community of interests (Pastor 2001; see also Hakim and Litan 2002; Chambers and Smith 2002). Brigham Young University Canadianist Earl Fry noted in a recent paper that "North-south integration is continuing to expand and deepen in areas far away from the respective national capitals. It will be interesting to observe whether there is sufficient national political will to formalize by treaty what is already occurring in the private sector and among many of the state and provincial governments in the three North American nations" (2003, 22; see also Weintraub 1994). Former US ambassador to Canada, Tom Niles, now president of the US Council for International Business, told a Calgary audience that "we ought to try to look at a customs union" (Scotton 2002). Baylor University economist Joe McKinney has analyzed the pros and cons of moving toward a deeper integration agreement and concludes that, while it would be difficult, both countries would benefit (2003). At the Washington-based Institute for International Economics, leading trade analysts Gary Hufbauer and Jeffrey Schott make the case for a serious look at a post-NAFTA trade and economic agenda (2004). Washington lawyer Patrick Macrory concludes that the NAFTA dispute settlement regime has worked well, but that there is scope for the two governments to work together on the basis of a series of incremental steps to make it work even better (2002).

Two parliamentary committees have also taken a first cut at defining the issues. The House of Commons Standing Committee on Foreign Affairs and International Trade, in its report of December 2002, provides a comprehensive survey of Canadian expert opinion, as well as some useful recommendations for immediate action, but it shies away from any recommendations that tackle broad strategic and economic issues. The Senate Standing Committee on Foreign Affairs (2003) proves even more reluctant to come to grips with the central issues affecting cross-border trade and investment. Both reports suffer from recording too many voices and engaging in too little analysis. As policy proposals become more refined, further hearings and analysis by parliamentary committees are likely, particularly hearings focused on specific options and opportunities.

The government has, to date, responded at best timidly to these reports, with the conspicuous exception of Pierre Pettigrew, the former minister of international trade.[17] In a little-noticed speech in Toronto on 18 October 2002, he outlined an inspired vision of the further evolution of Canada-US trade and economic relations. He set out six goals that add up to an ambitious agenda, which is unlikely to be achieved in the absence of serious negotiations to refine and upgrade the rules and institutions governing the shared Canada-US economic space. A year later he largely repeated the speech to another Toronto audience, but was able to announce progress on one of his key points: Canadian representation in the United States. A few weeks earlier, he and three colleagues announced a major increase in the number of consulates and trade offices Canada will maintain in the United States (2002, 2003a,b). Nevertheless, at a meeting of the NAFTA Commission in Montreal at the end of September 2003, Pettigrew and his colleagues were at pains to point out that the three partners, while exploring options to strengthen NAFTA and reduce the protectionist effect of rules of origin, were not contemplating the negotiation of a customs union.[18]

His colleague, Foreign Minister Bill Graham, tried valiantly at the annual Couchiching Conference to "have his cake and eat it too" on the issue of Canada-US integration. In a speech that would have done Mackenzie King proud, he told his audience that "we need to keep an eye on both the advantages and potential limitations of continental integration. And as we do so, we must guard against both simplistic views of what defines our sovereignty and simplistic views of what matters most to Canadians" (2003). Integration if necessary, but not necessarily integration. The pursuit of Canadian economic and security interests with the United States needs to be carefully balanced against the maintenance of Canadian values.

Former Finance Minister John Manley has at times proven to be a lone voice in the wilderness, trying to add some realism to his colleagues' understanding of the imperatives of Canada-US relations. In both speeches and unguarded moments with the press, he has made clear his impatience with those Canadians who espouse values but are unprepared to back them up with action and resources. In his brief campaign for the Liberal leadership, he made a valiant effort to place Canada-US relations at the centre of his campaign.

In his first few months in office, Prime Minister Paul Martin has signaled that refurbishing relations with the United States is high on his agenda. He is chairing a Cabinet committee on Canada-US relations and has appointed his parliamentary secretary, Scott Brison, to focus on the Canada-US file. Both are constructive signals of necessary changes to come. Even more important, however, is getting a handle on the objective, purpose and content of refurbished relations. A top priority in this respect will be to restore maturity and perspective to Canadian foreign policy in all its ramifications and to place Canada-US relations squarely at the centre, and on that basis to consider the challenges posed by deepening integration.

Unlike debate on the pros and cons of freer bilateral trade in the 1980s, discussion today is more broadly focused on the governance of shared North American economic and security concerns and includes consideration of defence, security, immigration and foreign policy issues as well as trade and investment. A broad consensus about the best way to proceed, if at all, remains elusive. Most commentators are agreed, however, that Canadians must first have a clear idea of what they want and why they want it before any useful dialogue can be initiated with the United States. Even American commentators, less concerned about bilateral issues than their northern cousins, accept the conventional wisdom that initiatives should originate in Canada, recognizing that Canadian sensitivities are likely to reach a fever pitch in response to any US initiatives.

American Interests

This conventional wisdom in Canada-US relations remains true and helps to explain the greater number of Canadian over US analysts engaged in developing new integration proposals. Nevertheless, this asymmetry in analysis should not be interpreted as denoting an absence of US interest. There are American interests, but they are not of the same order as those of Canada.[19] Cross-border integration has created a deep, and asymmetrical, dependence by Canadians on the US market. This market now takes more than 85 percent of Canadians' exports of goods and services; US firms supply about 65 percent of Canadian imports; US exports to Canada constitute about 24 percent of US exports while imports from Canada make up about 20 percent of the US import market. As a share of total US economic activity and consumption, however, Canadian exports amount to less than 3 percent of US consumption and Canadian imports a little over 2 percent of US production. In comparison, US exports satisfy about 35 percent of total Canadian demand and exports to the United States reflect about 40 percent of Canadian production (Department of Foreign Affairs and International Trade 2003).

The asymmetry is even more pronounced today than a generation earlier: in nominal terms, the US economy is 13 times the size of the Canadian economy; bilateral trade is about 18 times more important to Canadians than to Americans. US foreign direct investment (FDI) in Canada is valued at about 10 percent of total US FDI, while Canadian FDI in the United States represents about half of total Canadian FDI. Viewed from the host country, US foreign direct investment in Canada represents about 64 percent of the total, while Canadian FDI in the United States amounts to less than 10 percent of the total. The asymmetries in military power, cultural projection and a host of other indicators are too well known to Canadians to need repetition.

These asymmetries in direct economic interests disposes some Canadians to conclude that the United States government would not be interested in addressing the contours of a new accommodation with Canada. The evidence for this pessimistic conclusion is not convincing. In the first place, throughout the 1990s, Canada was a better US customer than were Europe or Japan. Canadians buy nearly three times as many goods and services from US suppliers as does Japan, and nearly twice the goods and services exported to Mexico. Canada is a reliable, cash customer and the number one foreign supplier of energy to the US market, including oil, gas, electricity and uranium, as well as a range of other commodities and manufactures. Canada is also a constant partner in pursuing an open, rules-based trade regime; over the past 65 years, no other country has been as consistently and creatively at the forefront in establishing the international trade order so highly valued by US officials.

The absolute value of US economic interest in a comprehensive trade and investment initiative is also roughly equal to that of Canada, but because its relative value is not and US international economic interests are more widely dispersed around the globe, US political leaders will need to be convinced of the wider implications of allowing deepening integration to become hostage to rules and procedures that have reached their past due date. A comprehensive Canada-US bilateral trade, investment and security initiative would provide a unique basis for resolving a wide range of issues between Canada and the United States that will strengthen Canada's attractiveness as an investment location to serve the Canadian, North

American and world markets, while addressing the urgent need to buttress security against terrorist and other transnational threats. Failure to tackle these issues will have a subtle, harmful impact on investor confidence in the Canadian economy — at home, in the United States and abroad — and on US security interests.

Most importantly, the United States has a vital interest in a relationship with Canada built on mutual trust and confidence, as does Canada. A more open and prosperous North America is, in the final analysis, the best guarantor of US and Canadian security. The tragic events of 11 September 2001 strengthened the case for a comprehensive initiative, adding an urgency to the security dimension that, in the post-Cold-War era, had faded from public consciousness. Disruptions at the border underlined to a growing number of Canadians and Americans the necessity of keeping the border open as a conduit for trade, tourism and investment and making it less vulnerable to disruption by terrorist and other threats. Both Canadian and American economic and security interests are clearly implicated in the free flow of goods and services between the two countries and in co-operative police, intelligence and related security strategies.

Political and Other Factors

PROCEEDING TOWARD ANY NEW INTEGRATION ARRANGEMENT SUITED TO THE NEEDS and circumstances of Canada and the United States will, of course, have implications that go beyond trade and commercial considerations. Some Canadians, for example, are concerned that closer commercial ties might drag them into pursuing US foreign policy goals that are inimical to Canadian interests.[20] Others worry that closer trade and commercial integration could undermine federal and provincial governments' ability to nurture Canadian culture and identity or to maintain Canada's approach to health care and regional development.[21] Still others fear that further negotiations could require Canada to share its resources and leave Canadians without an adequate capacity to ensure that they benefit from these assets. Some Canadians are suspicious that governments' approach to health care, education, regional development and other defining policies could be compromised.

These are serious concerns to which there are serious answers. Some of these fears relate more to the forces of proximity than to the nature of the rules in place to manage the flow of goods, services, capital, technology and people across the border.[22] Canadians can do little about the fact that they live next door to the world's largest, most energetic economy, but the negotiation of better rules and the establishment of more flexible institutions could provide an improved basis for managing the frictions created by proximity and ensure that Canadians are able to reap the full benefits of their geography. Other concerns are matters that would need to be addressed with care in the negotiation of the terms and conditions that would apply. There is no reason, for example, why Canada needs to change the goals embedded in its cultural or telecommunications policies to achieve a new accommodation with the United States, but there may be a need to reconsider the details of how they are implemented.

Like Canadians, Americans have worries that must be addressed. The essence of any negotiation involves resolving such issues and finding mutually acceptable terms. Without engaging, the natural tendency is to drift toward US-determined default positions. In order to address issues co-operatively and to the two countries' mutual benefit, the two governments must engage each other, analyze the issues as they emerge, and determine what can be accommodated and what cannot.

Before proceeding to an analysis of the principal agenda items that would need to be addressed in any deeper economic integration arrangements, seven political issues in particular need to be placed in context: the issue of sovereignty, the "erosion" of policy autonomy, worries about a "race to the bottom," the need to measure all the costs and benefits before proceeding, the relationship between any new bilateral arrangement and the multilateral rules of the World Trade Organization (WTO), concerns about "putting all our eggs in the US basket" and the place of Mexico in any negotiation.

Sovereignty

In considering the pros and cons of any deeper integration arrangements, some Canadians believe that any further steps will entail unacceptable sacrifices of Canadian sovereignty. To this claim, there is no better response than that offered by Hugh Segal. He said:

> Sovereignty is a vital national instrument. It is not a goal. We use it to shape domestic policy within our own borders; we share and divide sovereignty in the creation and negotiation of federal and confederal constitutions; we protect

> it through the patrol of our airspace, landmass, sea lanes and coastal waters with our armed forces, and we use it to make agreements with other sovereign nations duly and democratically elected Canadian governments deem to be in our national interest. Sovereignty is not hoarded, it is not locked away, it is there to be used to advance the legitimate social and economic interests of Canadians on a host of fronts. (Segal 2002)

In a similar vein, Wendy Dobson reminds Canadians that "sovereignty is not just about what a country gives up but also about what it gains in more efficient production, larger markets, freer flow of investment, swift resolution of disputes and greater protection of intellectual property, to name but a few of the benefits...States are the architects of their own constraints through the decisions they make...and through the decisions they avoid by failing to *exercise* their sovereignty" (Dobson 2002, 3).[23]

All international agreements, of course, whether aimed at economic, environmental, human rights, military, or other objectives, seek to curb the full expression of autonomous national decision-making. States make the reasonable calculation that their interests are better served if other states are required to behave in a predictable and stable manner, subject to commonly agreed rules and procedures to enforce them. Trade agreements are neither an exception to nor fundamentally different from the many other agreements, conventions and declarations to which Canada is party.[24]

Over the past six decades, Canada has been a pre-eminent leader in promoting, negotiating and accepting a rules- and regime-based system for the conduct of international relations. The driver of Canadian rule-making and institution-building is Canada's perception of itself as a country whose most intimate foreign relations are with powerful countries that, unrestrained, will take little account of, or may even damage, Canadian interests. Hence, the instinct to resolve problems through international rules and regimes has been a constant factor throughout the range of Canadian foreign-policy endeavours.

An integral component of this activist diplomacy has been a readiness to accept increasingly more stringent limits on the scope for autonomous decision-making, particularly in relations with the United States, in return for increased discipline on our foreign partners. The pursuit of more demanding forms of bilateral co-operation flows logically from earlier efforts. Deepening bilateral integration with the United States, in particular, challenges the two governments to take further steps down the mutually beneficial road of exercising their sovereignty to achieve important economic and other objectives.

Erosion of Policy Autonomy

A variant of the sovereignty concern is the worry about policy autonomy. Again, policy autonomy is not an end in itself, but a vital tool of governance. Whether governments achieve their goals and objectives autonomously or co-operatively is less important than their ability to serve the needs and aspirations of their citizens. As discussed in greater detail below, Canadian and American officials have developed extensive, mutually beneficial networks of co-operation and they work increasingly within the confines of internationally agreed rules and procedures. The reason is simple. Such co-operative, joint strategies are an efficient way to meet Canadian goals and to ensure that others behave in ways that protect and reflect Canadian interests (Doern, Pal, and Tomlin 1996; Banting, Hoberg, and Simeon 1997).

A further variant of this concern is the belief that much of what Canada needs to do can be done without reference to the United States. Canada can make such changes in its laws, policies and procedures as it deems desirable as a way of ensuring better and more secure access to the US market. Regulatory rapprochement with the United States, for example, can in many instances be achieved unilaterally. There is some truth to this assertion, but the will required for Canada to make such changes is often lacking and is easier to find in the context of negotiations that provide scope for trade-offs. US trust and confidence in Canada as a regulatory partner is also greatly enhanced by the exercise of working together to resolve common problems. Similarly, Canadian confidence in US willingness to maintain reliable access to its market is critically dependent on enshrining co-operative solutions in a treaty relationship. As an Industry Canada survey of Canadian regulators notes: "All of those surveyed indicated that their broad policy objectives were similar to those of their US counterparts. However, many stressed that differences in the respective systems of government and authorizing legislation complicate efforts to co-operate, effectively limiting what can be achieved without significant legislative changes." The same survey also indicated that "most co-operation takes place at the operational level" (Industry Canada 2002). At the same time, as the survey notes, without an external prod such as trade negotiations, regulatory co-operation among those operationally responsible quickly grinds to a halt; without the involvement of regulators in the negotiations, however, the objectives and means may not be well framed, leading to suboptimal results.

Canada, like many other advanced industrial countries, has learned the lesson that without the constraint of jointly agreed external rules, it is difficult to resist domestic protectionist interests. Throughout much of their history, Canadians have found it hard to accept that a resource-based economy without secure markets for its products, coupled with an inefficient, import-substitution manufacturing sector, provided a poor basis for sustained growth and prosperity. In the face of stubborn protectionism in the United States and in Europe, however, Canadians found it difficult to reduce foreign barriers to their exports or to resist the call for protection from their own manufacturers.

Canada now has one of the most open economies in the world, next door to the world's largest and most dynamic market. The deployment of sensible trade policies has gradually provided Canadians with the prosperity, the jobs and the choices that make the best of Canada's comparative advantage and allows them to reap the benefits of the best that others can offer. The challenge for the future is to protect, preserve and enhance these achievements, and to avoid retreating into the protectionist past that retarded attainment of these benefits.

"Race to the Bottom" and Similar Concerns

A frequently voiced criticism of deepening economic integration is that it will foster a "race to the bottom," that is, a relentless effort by governments to attract foreign investors and retain domestic investors by reducing regulatory norms and expectations. There is little evidence to support this claim. Indeed, there is a preponderance of evidence pointing in exactly the opposite direction.[25] As societies become more prosperous — one of the most important impacts of liberalization and deepening integration — the demand for regulations to enhance the quality of life increases. The explosion of government regulatory activity to address environmental, social, human rights, safety and other issues provides compelling evidence of the gap between rhetoric and reality. In the other direction, the impact of regulatory convergence and regulatory co-operation has been repeatedly to raise the bar by establishing international benchmarks of minimal performance and best international practice. Despite populist notions to the contrary, US regulatory requirements are often more stringent than those in Canada. More to the point, bilateral regulatory convergence is more likely to involve adoption of best practices than reliance on the most common denominator.

Measuring Costs and Benefits

In the lead-up to Canada's decision in 1985 to pursue free trade with the United States, Donald Macdonald indicated that Canadians would need to take "a leap of faith." His remarks were widely reported and misunderstood. His point was a very simple one: not all outcomes are fully knowable in advance. Like today's critics of deeper integration, the Cassandras of the 1980s worried that not enough studies had been done that demonstrated the extent of the costs and benefits of free trade. The volumes of learned articles explaining — both theoretically and empirically — the benefits of freer trade, were not sufficient. What was needed, critics insisted, were studies that would demonstrate specific outcomes and precise costs and benefits to the Canadian economy. Today's skeptics call for detailed studies examining costs and benefits of deepening integration to various sectors of the economy. Such studies, to the extent that data are available and that researchable questions can be posed, may prove useful, but in the final analysis they can do no more than sketch probabilities. To paraphrase Yogi Berra, the trouble with predicting the future is that you do not always know where you are headed or what detours may be in store. Nevertheless, as discussed further below, while entering negotiations to forge new arrangements to govern deepening bilateral integration may require a leap of faith, it need not involve a leap in the dark. Extensive analysis exists examining various scenarios.

Erosion of Canada's Multilateral Commitments

Given the widely held view asserting Canada's strong multilateralist heritage, some analysts continue to express concern that further bilateral steps will undermine Canada's ability to benefit from multilateral negotiations, and will further weaken efforts to find multilateral solutions.[26] Such analysts confuse ends and means.[27] Multilateral rule-making and institution-building have proven effective means for Canada to pursue its trade and other objectives, including with the United States. Bilateral rules and institutions have complemented and will continue to complement these efforts. Both should be judged on their ability to satisfy Canadian needs and interests. Additionally, such analysts ignore the fact that the multilateral regime has, from the beginning, included provisions that recognize that governments will pursue their objectives by more than one means (Hart 1996). To date, WTO members have notified the organization of more than 200 bilateral and regional arrangements under its terms.

Canada and the United States have already implemented a WTO-consistent regional trade agreement. Impediments to deepening their commitments raised by WTO rules are minimal to non-existent. They can, for example, craft aspects of a customs union on a sector-by-sector basis without ever making a formal declaration or notification to the WTO that they have decided to create a customs union. More generally, Canada and the United States need to conclude an agreement that serves their needs and catches up to the reality of deepening integration, and only worry about the WTO rules in the final stages of any negotiation. As was their experience during the CUFTA negotiations, the international rules are a useful guide, not a constraining force.

Deepening bilateral commitments beyond NAFTA may require the two governments to develop a common approach to the treatment of trade and investment with third parties, including third parties with which either or both countries have negotiated free trade agreements. The most important such partner is Mexico. Should Canada and the United States pursue deeper integration arrangements, they will need to pay particular attention to their impact on Mexico. This is more a matter of the political economy of North America than of the WTO rules. As Europe has demonstrated during its long trip along the integration path, it is possible to forge a variety of relationships with different partners, reflecting different needs, goals and circumstances.[28]

It is also important to keep in mind that multilateral negotiations are extremely time consuming and the final product must, of necessity, reflect the lowest common denominator acceptable to the key players. While brave pronouncements about broad objectives and ambitious time frames have become part of the ritual of launching and sustaining such negotiations, experience over the past three decades suggests that each new round of multilateral trade negotiations has taken longer, involved more players, focused on a larger and more complex agenda and strayed further and further from issues of greatest import to Canada-US deepening integration. The current Doha Development Round of WTO negotiations is no exception. For Canada, as has always been the case, self-interest dictates a pragmatic mix of means in pursuing its most pressing priorities (Hart 2002/03).

Putting All Our Eggs in the US Basket

Some Canadians are concerned about Canada putting all its eggs in the US basket and failing to pay attention to Canada's many interests around the world. They miss the point. It is not Canada, but Canadians, who are driving the process of deepening bilateral integration. Canada, the country, does not trade despite frequent claims to the contrary by ministers and their officials. Trade flows from the impact of billions of discrete and seemingly unrelated decisions by individuals in their daily decisions about what to eat, wear, drive, read and otherwise spend their resources. Overwhelmingly, those choices favour North American products. US markets and suppliers are now the overwhelming preference of Canadian firms and individuals, and Canadian markets and suppliers have assumed a growing importance to US firms and consumers. The pace of this process accelerated perceptibly in the 1980s, to the benefit of both Canadians and Americans, creating the conditions that underpinned deepening integration in the 1990s.

Calls for "diversifying" Canada's trade relations fly in the face of these emerging patterns and make little economic sense (Dymond and Hart 2002). Ever since Prime Minister Trudeau pursued his failed "third option" of trade diversification in the 1970s, a small segment of Canadians have continued to be worried by the "threat" of Canada's growing integration into the North American economy. As a matter of fact, Canadian trade — exports and imports — is already highly diversified. The range of products and suppliers vying for consumer attention has increased dramatically over the past decades, while Canadian producers service millions of customers. Most of them happen to be in North America, because that is where the most profitable opportunities are to be found.

Are there profitable opportunities beyond North America that Canadian firms would like to service but can't because of trade barriers? The evidence is not persuasive. As a result of nearly seven decades of trade negotiations, the markets of most of the industrialized countries are on the whole open. The remaining barriers are of two types: those protecting the most sensitive — read politically potent — sectors, and regulatory and structural barriers that are much more difficult to tackle. Multilateral and regional trade negotiations will chip away at both. Canadians should make every effort to reduce and eliminate such barriers, just as they should be prepared to reduce any constraints on access to their own market. They need to do that because it makes good economic sense, not because of some ephemeral and unachievable goal of diversification.

There is, of course, an alternative. The Canadian government could start telling businesses where to trade, investors where to invest and consumers what to buy. Other governments would have to act in the same way by interfering in the choices of their consumers and investors — the United States, for example, by throwing up barriers to Canadian exports, and the Europeans by lowering their remaining obstacles to Canadian trade. The result would inevitably be more diversified trade, but at considerably diminished volumes that generated fewer jobs and lower incomes. For the great mass of Canadians who earn their living from working in the private economy, this would be path of lunacy, a path Canadians overwhelmingly and sensibly reject.

The Mexico Dimension

In concluding NAFTA in 1993, Canada and the United States opened a new era in their relations with Mexico. The NAFTA stands as testimony to the belief that the North American community involves three nations and that the destiny of all three nations is inextricably intertwined. Broad consensus is emerging, however, that for the moment the Canadian challenge is to elaborate a bilateral rather than a trilateral agenda.[29] Successful implementation of NAFTA ushered in expectations of closer trilateral relations, but the reality is that NAFTA provides a common framework of rules to govern two robust and rapidly evolving relationships: between the United States and Canada and between the United States and Mexico. Canada-Mexico relations remain at a much less advanced stage, while the priority issues between Canada and the United States and Mexico and the United States are not of the same order. There are issue areas where there may already be scope for advancing toward trilateral rules and institutions, for example, surface transportation, while in other issue areas much more will be gained from parallel bilateral efforts, for example, energy. To that end, the three governments may wish to consider pursuing ways and means to network any bilateral efforts and ensure that success at the bilateral level ultimately feeds into trilateral goals and aspirations.[30]

Emerging Patterns of Canada-US Cross-Border Trade and Production

IN 1980, TWO-WAY BILATERAL TRADE IN GOODS AND SERVICES REPRESENTED ABOUT 40 percent of Canadian gross domestic product (GDP). Two decades later, that figure had nearly doubled to reach about 75 percent, valued at some C$700 billion annually or $2 billion every day.[31] Two-way flows of foreign direct investment have similarly reached new highs: in the early 1980s, the value of annual two-way flows averaged under $10 billion. By 2000, they had reached $340 billion, and reflected a much greater balance between US- and Canada-originating flows.[32] In 2002, some 11 million trucks, or about 30,000 per day, crossed the border to carry much of this trade; the Ambassador Bridge between Windsor and Detroit alone handles over 7,000 trucks a day, or one every minute in each direction, 24 hours a day; about 100,000 passenger vehicles also cross the Canada-US border every day, in addition to millions of tons of freight carried by planes, railcars, ships and pipelines. Over 200 million individual crossings now take place at the Canada-US border annually, an average of more than half a million every day. On average, 15 million Canadians — of a population of 31 million — travel annually to the United States for visits of more than one day to conduct business, break up the long winter, visit friends and relatives or otherwise pursue legitimate objectives, while slightly fewer Americans visit Canada for similar reasons.

Since 9/11 and the slowdown in the US economy, growth in bilateral trade has not kept pace with the impressive rate set over much of the 1990s. The impact of enhanced security at the border has added to increased concern about the efficacy of serving the North American market from the Canadian side of the border. Combined with inevitable congressional and administrative protectionism in the face of the US recession, these factors suggest that a return to the robust post-FTA/NAFTA numbers will require, at a minimum, serious government attention to remaining and new barriers and impediments. More importantly, as the analysis will suggest, more fundamental factors need to be considered in order to design bilateral policies, arrangements and institutions that will pay long-term dividends.

Historically, deepening Canada-US economic integration has been driven by private market behaviour which, in turn, has shaped the nature of the policy response. While deepening patterns of trade and investment now point to the need for further policy responses, it is also important that the policy responses be consonant with the changing nature of the cross-border pull of trade and investment. Canadian producers and consumers are now much more integrated into international supply lines. John Curtis has written that over the past 20 years Canadian manufacturers have more than doubled their reliance on export markets. Canada is now much more than a resource economy (2003).

Trade policy and trade agreements from the 1930s through the 1970s were largely designed to eliminate or discipline barriers to exchanges between unrelated parties operating in two separate markets. Such cross-border transactions are increasingly the exception. Starting with the 1965 Autopact, the two governments have sought to address barriers to much more integrative trade and, increasingly, investment. Today, more than two-thirds of cross-border trade is between related parties, taking place either wholly within the confines of a single firm or among parties to an integrated network of firms. A third of the value of Canada's total exports today is made up of previously imported inputs (Cross 2002). The typical automobile, for example, assembled in Canada and exported to the United States, is made up of inputs that may already have crossed the border up to five times as they wended their way up the value chain. Just-in-time production strategies involve an intricate pattern of parts and components flowing from one plant to another; freer trade has made it possible for firms to locate such plants strategically throughout North America, with less and less regard for borders. The automotive sector is the most integrated, but other sectors are rapidly catching up, and even resource trade is seeing new patterns of integration. Nevertheless, the continued presence of borders and regulatory differences also shapes such decisions, often to the detriment of locations in Canada.[33]

Traditional trade agreements also assumed that trade was largely a matter of exchanging goods and that the production of goods was the mainstay of economic growth and development. Today, three-quarters of North Americans are employed in delivering services; manufacturing now directly employs fewer than one in five workers in both countries; and manufacturing directly contributes less than one-fifth to either country's GDP. More than one-fifth of the value of *recorded* trade transactions now involves the exchange of services. Value derived from licensing, investments and other nongoods transactions have also become more critical to cross-border economic linkages. An unknown, but growing, share of value is added on the basis of electronic transactions that take place within the proprietary networks of integrated firms with operations on both sides of the border, little of which is either recorded as trade or generally recognized as part of deepening patterns of cross-border linkages.[34]

These emerging patterns of integration are market responses to opportunities created by technological developments. Liberalization embedded in intergovernmental agreements, however, helped to create the environment within which these opportunities proved profitable. The benefits of that liberalization have now been largely realized in trade between Canada and the

United States. The issues that now condition much more varied trade and investment patterns are less classic market segmenting policies such as tariffs and quotas, and more subtle regulatory differences. Border administration remains important to the enforcement of these differences, but the key to addressing them is less a matter of liberalization and more a matter of designing a co-operative or co-ordinated approach to governance of the market. In short, in North America, the trade policy of shallow integration based on liberalization is giving way to the challenge of forging rules for deep integration. The focus of liberalization agreements was largely static rule-making centred on the cross-border movement of goods; the focus of deep integration agreements revolves around much more dynamic institutions and procedures affecting a more varied range of cross-border transactions, including the movement of all the factors of production.

Stages of Integration

British economist David Henderson defines integration "as a tendency for the economic significance of political boundaries to diminish" (1994, 179-80). Deepening integration between two or more countries thus disposes them to create common policies to regulate the production and distribution of goods and services and a joint approach to external trade and investment.[35] Integration stems from two basic forces: the "push" of public policy efforts to reduce the impact of borders and other government-imposed barriers to the freer flow of the factors of production, and the "pull" of private firms' behaviour in responding to market opportunities. The two forces can be either complementary or adversarial. Governments can either facilitate or retard the commercial impact of proximity, consumer choice and business judgement. The pace of integration can flow either from the push of government action or the pull of firm behaviour, or both.

In terms of international policy commitments, most-favoured-nation treatment and preferential-trade liberalization usually involve little more than commitments to bind and reduce tariff levels, and to implement a code of rules and good practices to govern the application of other instruments of commercial policy such as quantitative restrictions, subsidies and customs procedures. Such agreements typically focus on border measures that apply to trade in goods. The GATT is the best-known example of a multilateral, rules-based trade-liberalization agreement, while the series of arrangements Canada forged with Commonwealth trading partners in the first half of the twentieth century are examples of preferential liberalization.

Establishing a free trade area marks a further stage of integration, requiring the participating governments to remove tariffs and eliminate or circumscribe as many other restrictions on cross-border commerce as possible.[36] Historically, most free-trade-area agreements have been limited to trade in goods and have focused on border measures. A complicating characteristic of free trade areas is the need for rules of origin to distinguish the goods originating in the territory of the parties, and thus eligible for "area" treatment, from those originating in third countries. Chapters 3 through 12 of CUFTA provide a classic example of a thorough free trade agreement. The provisions set out in the chapters on services, investment, temporary business travel and financial services went well beyond the contours of a conventional free trade agreement.

The next stage, a customs union, involves establishment of a common external trade policy and a single customs territory, allowing for the free circulation of all goods within the customs union.[37] It requires the parties to harmonize their tariff and other customs policies; develop a common approach to antidumping, countervailing and similar procedures; consider full reciprocity in the administration of government procurement regulations; pursue such instruments as mutual recognition agreements to reduce the impact of regulatory differences; and orchestrate a range of similar policies to ensure the free circulation of goods, and perhaps services, between them and a common approach to trade in goods with third parties.

A common market, the next stage of regional integration, builds on a customs union and, in addition, allows for the free circulation of all factors of production: goods, services, capital, technology and people. To effect a common market between them, participating governments would, in addition to implementing the tasks required to create a customs union, need to address impediments to the free flow of services, capital, technology and people. The first three aspects normally do not create insuperable obstacles but do require the parties to resolve some difficult issues, including differences in regulatory regimes such as competition and securities laws. The free movement of people presents perhaps the most daunting task. In Europe, the 1985 Schengen Agreement, negotiated many years after the Common Market came into force, finally gave full effect, in 1990, to the commitment to free circulation of people among its signatories. The United Kingdom and Ireland still do not participate fully in the Schengen accord.

The most ambitious approach along this continuum of integrative arrangements is an economic union, involving a common currency and common approaches to macroeconomic policies. The European Union, over its 50-year trajectory, has moved from a customs union to a common market and, finally in 1993, to an economic union. Full economic union, however, has not yet been achieved among all 15 member states — the UK, for example, has not as yet adopted the common currency or the Schengen accord — and is likely to slow somewhat as a result of the accession of 10 new members in 2004.

To function effectively, customs unions, common markets and economic unions require sufficiently robust institutions to implement the detailed rules required to govern these arrangements. The success of Europe's progressively more integrative arrangements depended to a considerable degree on the willingness of the member states to invest both the supranational institutions: the European Commission, the European Court and the European Parliament, and the intergovernmental institutions: the Presidency and the Council of Ministers, with increasing authority or "competence." Europe's institution-rich environment operates on the basis of very detailed treaties, arrangements and protocols that reflect, to some extent, the civil law traditions of most of the members of the European Union. It is not surprising that the United Kingdom, with its rich common law heritage, has been the least enthusiastic participant in the European integration process.

As the above description suggests, Canada and the United States, while nominally committed to no more than a free trade area, have in reality already implemented aspects of a customs union and even of a common market. Based on broadly shared goals and perspectives and common needs, the two governments have developed a dense framework of formal and informal networks and relationships that ensures a high degree of convergence in the design and implementation of a wide range of rules and regulations. Indeed, the degree of informal macroeconomic concertation between the two federal governments has long been more advanced than that in Europe on the eve of the decision to implement the European Economic Union.

The European Experience Holds Limited Lessons for Canada and the United States

THE PUSH OF GOVERNMENT ACTION, BASED ON NON-ECONOMIC OBJECTIVES, HAS BEEN critical to European integration. The establishment of first the European Coal and Steel Community in 1952 and then the Common Market in 1958 revolved to a considerable extent around efforts to create a firmer economic base for promoting peace and security, particularly between France and Germany.[38] The original four smaller players eagerly supported efforts to maintain good relations between these two powers. It has since evolved into three major players — France, Germany and the United Kingdom — with major ambitions that need frequently to be fed to keep the Union intact, at least eight players that continue to be strongly committed to the original goal of sustaining peace and harmony on a Europe-wide basis, and a group of four southern members. The addition of ten new members in 2004 is again predicated on using economic means to achieve the political end of solidifying democracy and market economics.[39]

The European approach was also fully consistent with the economic and security needs identified in the 1940s and 1950s and the reality of more than two dozen fully independent states, many with long traditions of keeping their markets closed to each other and a wide range of ingenious devices to meet this goal. It took more than 30 years and a high level of will, co-operation, and institution-building to create what has become known as the *acquis communautaires,* the very detailed construction of rules that now governs the conduct of affairs within the Union. The outline of that policy was set by the original six members, and subsequent members accepted the framework adopted in the 1950s. There may be interesting lessons at the level of specific policies that may usefully be studied, but the broad approach chosen to effect European integration was unique to Europe's circumstances.

Rather than the European push of government action, North American integration has been largely driven by the pull of market forces: proximity, consumer choice, investment preference and firm behaviour. Government policy has been largely responsive, motivated by efforts to resolve problems generated by commercially driven integration. Rather than seeking deeper integration, governments have only gradually accepted the need to facilitate it by addressing problems experienced by private traders and investors. The result is a much more piecemeal and less deliberate approach to rule-making and institution-building.

The European experience also reflects the capacity of governments with strong central executives responsible to multiparty parliaments to enter into and manage co-operative strategies. None of the member states is governed on the basis of a decentralized, congressional-presidential system with all of its built-in checks and balances. When European leaders meet to iron out differences, they are fully competent to enact and implement the results of their discussions. The highly fragmented American decision-making process, on the other hand, makes it very difficult for the central authority to exercise much supervision over the rule-making activities of the states and even of some of the quasi-independent commissions established by Congress. The US president, for example, may appoint the commissioners to the Securities and Exchange Commission, but once in office, they act fully independently of his direction. Similarly, the federal government in Canada, while it controls its own agenda, cannot direct the provinces in areas of provincial jurisdiction. While it would be possible to conceive of a bilateral agreement that would subject all regulatory decision-making to its rules, procedures and institutions, such an agreement would be very difficult to negotiate and even more difficult to implement and manage. As experience has demonstrated, even the much less intrusive CUFTA and NAFTA have at times proved unequal to the challenge of bringing some well-entrenched US state or federal institutions or Canadian provincial institutions into line.

At the same time, it is important to keep in mind that the pull of silent, market-led integration has already created a degree of policy and regulatory convergence between the two federal governments, and among the states and provinces, that considerably eases the task of finding ways and means to strengthen bilateral co-operation in the governance of the integrated North American economic space. Similarly, it is no accident that, to some extent, CUFTA and NAFTA, while billed as free trade areas largely because of tariff and related programs, already involve elements of a customs union and even a common market but also lack some critical elements. The provisions governing the flow of both services and investment, as well as those related to temporary business travel, go well beyond the requirements of a free trade area and anticipate elements of a common market. Finally, Canada and the United States have the advantage — as a result of the impact of silent integration and nearly 70 years of bilateral and multilateral negotiations — of close convergence in external tariff levels, a deeply embedded commitment to national treatment, and extensive convergence in regulatory purpose and design.

Challenges to Further Cross-Border Integration

The Canada-US border has always been a critical conditioning factor in Canadian economic development. In many ways, a recurring theme in Canadian trade policy and negotiations has been either to enhance or offset the impact of the border (Hart 2002). Initially, Canada sought to increase investment by creating a captive, protected market. The result was a larger economy but a poorer Canada.[40] Since the 1930s, Canada has sought to attract investment to serve world markets, particularly US markets. To an investor, serving the North American market from inside the larger US market makes intuitive sense. In response, a constant goal of Canadian trade policy has thus been to strive to offset this natural investor bias. Reducing the border effect is critical to this effort.

Despite seven decades of multilateral, regional and bilateral trade and investment negotiations, however, barriers to the efficient cross-border movement of capital, technology, services, goods and people continue to exist. The high levels of current trade reflect considerable success in reducing barriers to mutually beneficial exchanges, but remaining barriers are by no means insignificant, particularly in the areas of goods and people.[41] A brief inventory of the terrain may be helpful in focusing the analysis.

To all intents and purposes, capital moves freely between the two countries, subject only to their similar regulatory regimes that address fiduciary, fiscal, competition and similar concerns. Differences in these regimes are, to a large extent, already benefiting from mutual recognition agreements, information-sharing arrangements, co-operative enforcement understandings and similar strategies. Further co-operative efforts along these lines, however, would yield additional beneficial results, particularly if they form part of a larger strategy.

Foreign direct investment, while generally subject to few restraints, remains restricted in a limited number of sectors, including national security, culture, telecommunications, transportation, energy and financial services. The scope for addressing these remaining restrictions is dependent on either or both governments either forgoing these objectives or accepting that the objectives served by these restrictions could be served by other means, often to greater effect.[42]

Restrictions on the cross-border exchange of technology have been reduced to a small number of national security-related objectives, most of which are in turn governed by a range of mutually satisfactory bilateral arrangements. Little remains to be done in this area.

Differences between the two countries' intellectual property regimes have, as a result of both NAFTA and the WTO TRIPS Agreement, been reduced to a minimum, and pose at most a minor obstacle to deepening bilateral integration. Such restrictions as remain would appear to be amenable to relatively straightforward arrangements based on mutual recognition and similar approaches.[43]

Trade in services is largely unencumbered by restrictions, either because such restrictions were never introduced or have been addressed in NAFTA or the WTO. Those that remain fall largely into four categories: professional certification requirements, restrictions on foreign direct investment, restrictions affecting cross-border movement of personnel, and limitations on government-provided services. The first is subject to an active, if unhurried, program of discussions to expand and facilitate accreditation on a cross-border basis. The second is covered by the discussion on FDI above. The third is part of broader immigration concerns discussed below. The fourth provides scope for some expansion in cross-border trade but is politically sensitive and not the subject of much commercial interest on either side of the border.

Cross-border movement of goods, while generally free, remains subject to an astonishing array of customs and regulatory requirements. These can be divided into two broad categories: those intended to discriminate in favour of either Canadian or US producers, and those that are the incidental result of regulations aimed at other objectives. The first represents the residual elements of traditional trade liberalization negotiations and includes such measures as tariffs on some agricultural products, remaining government procurement restrictions, trade remedy laws, and similar measures. The second involves a wide range of measures that reflect the increasing complexity of modern economies and the responses of governments to demands ranging from consumer protection to environmental stewardship. The cross-border effect of the first can be addressed with the traditional approach, but would benefit from some new ideas. The second requires an intense program of co-operation to identify those regulations that no longer serve any useful public purpose, those that can be implemented and administered on a basis that limits or eliminates the impact of differences, and those between which differences are profound and important. Only the latter may need to continue to create any substantive barriers to trade, but on a much more limited basis than is the case today.

The cross-border movement of people remains the most challenging area of border administration, challenges flowing largely from security concerns but also involving economic interests. Organized labour on both sides of the border, for example, continues to believe that freer cross-border movement of labour would have a negative impact on the interests of its members. As has been demonstrated by the experience in Europe, as well as under the CUFTA/NAFTA temporary entry provisions, there is little evidence to support this concern, but organized labour's more general opposition to freer trade indicates that any movement on this front will need to overcome this opposition. The nexus between the freer movement of people and security adds to the difficult agenda that must be addressed to make progress on this issue. Canadian and US immigration policy objectives and programs may be broadly similar, but co-operation among officials is less in evidence than in other areas (Rekai 2002). The scope for enhanced co-operation is broad while the payoff would be significant (Harris and Schmitt 2003).

Based on this survey, the most important trade and economic issues raised by deepening cross-border integration can be divided into four main areas:

Border administration. Administration of the physical border continues to involve a dense array of laws and procedures conditioning trade and investment decisions, including costs of compliance and the potential costs created by delays, not to mention infrastructure and administrative costs for the two governments. In the words of former trade minister, Pierre Pettigrew, the government needs "to keep pace with the demands and expectations of businesses on both sides of the border who rely on just-in-time delivery and easy access to markets" and move beyond current programs and approaches (2002, 5).

Regulatory differences. Both intergovernmental agreements and the pressures of silent integration have accelerated regulatory convergence and narrowed regulatory differences, but they have neither eliminated existing differences nor discouraged new, often small, differences in regulatory design, objectives, implementation and compliance from emerging, imposing costs and maintaining distortions in the operations of the two economies. As former Prime Minister Brian Mulroney told a Washington audience in December 2002, "Our economies are now closely connected and interdependent, a reality that needs to be better reflected in the way our governments manage our national affairs and in the way they regulate economic activity. They should work together to ensure that while our national systems of regulations serve to protect our citizens, and are fully respectful of our different constitutions, they are also as compatible as possible in order to increase the efficiency of our economies and enhance our global competitiveness" (2002).

Institutional capacity. Managing deepening integration and an increasingly complex relationship requires that the two governments assess the capacity of current institutional and procedural frameworks to iron out differences, reduce conflict and provide a more flexible basis for adapting to changing circumstances. In the words of Jean Monnet, the father of European integration, "nothing is possible without men; nothing is lasting without institutions" (1978, 304-05).

Contingency protection and resource pricing. Despite a decade and a half of free trade, the application of trade remedies in a few sectors continues to create tensions in the relationship. The extent of intracorporate and other structural forms of commercial integration has virtually eliminated resort to trade remedies by firms in the manufacturing and industrial sectors. Problems, however, persist in the natural resource and agricultural sectors. Many of these are related to different approaches to resource pricing, suggesting that an indirect approach to trade remedies — addressing the issues that give rise to complaints — may be more fruitful than further efforts to address the issue directly. As former Canadian ambassador to the United States, Derek Burney, points out, "in more and more products, Canadian and American firms are competing as one industry in a single, integrated market. Trade remedy laws should accommodate that reality"(2003a, 6).

The first three are inextricably intertwined. As discussed further below, regulatory differences are now the mainstay of border administration, while institutional capacity is critical to effecting greater regulatory convergence. Appreciating the extent to which these three issues are interrelated is critical to unravelling how Canada and the United States can work together to pursue their mutual interests in a more open and more secure North American economy. Contingency protection, on the other hand, is the most visible and difficult residual issue left over from earlier negotiations. The solution to this long-standing conundrum, however, may also lie in finding the best way to address regulatory co-operation and institutional capacity.

The Contours of a Deep Integration Agreement

In speeches delivered in the fall of 2002 and 2003, Pierre Pettigrew, then minister of international trade, outlined six goals "for the Canada we want in the North America we are building." He wanted to:

1. increase Canada's share of the US market;
2. strengthen two-way flows of investment in order to promote trade, technology flows, research and innovation;
3. advance an agenda of "smart" regulation with "a view to promoting health, encouraging innovation and economic growth and reducing the burden on business," by broadening and deepening regulatory co-operation and greater use of mutual recognition and less duplication and overlap;
4. bring trade remedy practice into "line with the growing integration of our shared North American economic space";
5. "eliminate the border as an impediment to trade, investment and business development and move the border away from the border," building on the momentum of the Smart Border Accord, but moving well beyond it; and
6. increase Canada's presence in the United States. (2002, 4; 2003b)

In sum, Pettigrew articulated an ambitious agenda fully in line with the growing pains experienced as a result of deepening and accelerating integration. To achieve these six points, however, more will be required than the incrementalism his speeches envisage. Canada and the United States will need to be prepared to put together a major program of co-operation and negotiation. In effect, his six points add up to a reasonable agenda for negotiating a deep integration agreement between the two countries. To work, such an agreement would need to include the following elements: (1) a common external tariff and related tariff programs; (2) an agreed approach to non-tariff customs treatment of third-country goods, including noncommercial restrictions on third-country trade such as foreign policy sanctions;

(3) steps to address remaining sectoral trade problems, particularly in agriculture; (4) an agreed approach to trade remedies for each other's products and/or for third-country products; (5) means to address bilateral restrictions on access to each other's government procurement markets; (6) ways and means to provide for the freer movement of people across the bilateral border and complementary steps to address the entry of people from outside North America; (7) a more active program of regulatory co-operation aimed at reducing overlap and duplication; (8) a new approach to border administration, consonant with the progress made on other issues and predicated on reducing, even eliminating, the impact of the border on most transactions and cross-border travel; and (9) appropriate institutional arrangements capable of addressing a much more dynamic and flexible approach to the governance of the two countries' common economic space.

The two governments can proceed to the negotiation of a comprehensive agreement from the start, or they can take a step-by-step approach, going as far as possible or necessary on individual issues. There are good reasons, however, to take a large, rather than a small, view from the start. The US political process is more readily engaged with a bold, visionary approach than a timid, incremental one. It has long been conventional wisdom among Canada-US watchers that for any major initiative to succeed, it needs to attract a high profile in the United States and maintain a low profile in Canada. In the American system, initiatives require a lot of political oxygen to survive and succeed, but in the Canada-US context, that very same oxygen is perceived to be too threatening to Canadian sensitivities, thus adding to the complexity of managing Canada-US relations.

While this wisdom still holds true for the way Washington works, as we saw above, Canadians are no longer as sensitive about their relationship with the United States as they may have been in the past. The 1990s may prove to have been a watershed in this regard, and the public reaction to the events of 9/11 certainly was indicative of a deep commitment to work with the United States to solve common problems and threats. Canadians no longer feel as threatened by their proximity to the United States and are more inclined to see this proximity as an opportunity, particularly on trade and economic matters. The failure of the dire predictions raised during the free trade debate of the 1980s to materialize seems to have exorcised the ghosts of earlier sensitivities.[44] Thus, fears about raising the profile of any new Canada-US initiatives seem to be grounded in an appreciation of most Canadians that is no longer valid.

The principal challenge to finding a more appropriate balance in the governance of deepening bilateral economic ties, therefore, lies as much in Washington as in Ottawa. As Allan Gotlieb explains, "for any initiative to succeed, it must meet a number of conditions. It must be bold, it must come from Canada and be espoused at the highest level. It must be comprehensive so as to allow trade-offs and broad constituencies to come into play. It must address the US agenda as well as ours. Incrementalism won't work" (2003b; see also Gotlieb 1991).

A Common Tariff and Related Tariff Programs

As a result of seven decades of bilateral and multilateral trade negotiations, Canada and the United States have succeeded in reducing the tariff to a residual instrument of industrial policy, critical to only a few categories of goods, particularly supply-managed dairy and poultry products in Canada and sensitive agricultural products such as peanuts, sugar, tobacco, cotton and wool in the United States. The remnants of what was once a major instrument of government policy, however, are sufficiently complex to require some careful consideration of what is involved in establishing a common tariff and related tariff programs.

In terms of the administrative dimensions of the tariff, the GATT and related negotiations have resulted in a high degree of convergence between the two countries' customs procedures, including customs valuation and reliance on the Harmonized System of tariff nomenclature (HS). There remain, however, some differences that would need to be addressed. Canada's customs tariff, for example, currently involves 6,821 industrial tariff lines, while that of the United States has 8,445. Some effort would need to be devoted to harmonizing beyond the six-digit level, as required by the HS, to the eight-digit level used by both countries, as permitted under the HS. It would largely require that Canada "break out" more items from six to eight digits to conform to US break-outs.

There is also a high level of convergence in rates. On approximately 3,000 tariff items, the two countries already impose the same most-favoured-nation (MFN) rate: zero. For about 40 percent of the remaining products, the difference is less than two percentage points, suggesting that the scope for harmonizing to the lowest rate applied by either country would not impose a major political hurdle.[45] The issues here are technical and administrative, not political.

The simplest and quickest way to achieve a common external tariff (CET), of course, is to increase the number of items subject to duty-free treatment on an

MFN basis. Establishing a Canada-US CET based, at least in part, on enlarging the scope for MFN free trade, as part of a bilateral customs union, would also provide an opportunity to exercise leadership on the multilateral front.[46] Problems, of course, exist, but they are limited to a relatively small number of sectors where the two countries maintain high rates, but not always on the same products. A useful point of departure here would be to harmonize those tariffs to the level of the lowest partner, but negotiate mutually acceptable rates for those few sectors and items for which this is not politically feasible. The goal, of course, would be to reduce this group to as small a list as possible.[47]

While the organizing principle for negotiating a common external tariff would be the MFN rate, the two governments would also need to address the various preferential rates maintained by the two countries. The general preferential tariff (GPT) rates in both countries assessed on goods from developing countries would need to be harmonized.[48] Again, a good point of departure would be to work from the default position of applying the lower of the two rates where they differ. Both countries maintain more generous (i.e., lower) rates for the least-developed countries and subsets of developing countries, but eligible goods and countries are not identical and it will thus require some effort to harmonize these lists. Again, moving to MFN free trade on as many items as possible is the best way to go, solving this issue as well as the next.

Both countries have negotiated, or are negotiating, free trade agreements with various countries.[49] There is some overlap in FTA partner countries, but the two lists are not identical. Again, efforts will have to be devoted to harmonizing these lists, including addressing differences in the coverage and rules for countries with which both have negotiated free trade agreements. While this task may be technically demanding, the relatively low levels of trade involved, actual and potential, suggests that the political impact will be relatively minor.

Preferential tariff rates require the application of rules of origin to distinguish between eligible and non-eligible goods. Canada's approach tends to be simpler than that of the United States, but with the conclusion of the Canada-US FTA and its introduction of the tariff-shift plus value-added approach, both countries have moved in this direction. Efforts to negotiate WTO disciplines to govern rules of origin, as anticipated by the Uruguay Round agreement on rules of origin, have not made much progress, but the technical work pursued at the WTO and at the World Customs Organization have laid useful foundations for further efforts at convergence. Establishing a CET would concentrate the minds of the officials involved, provide them with a more compelling strategic framework, and afford them further opportunity to show leadership. They could do so by negotiating a simpler set of rules to govern their common imports from GPT-eligible and FTA partner countries.

By establishing a CET, the need for rules of origin on cross-border trade would disappear. The complexity of these rules and the density of Canada-US trade suggests that the transaction cost of complying with rules of origin is significant. Various studies suggest that, on average, they impose the equivalent of a 2 to 3 percent tax on cross-border transactions sensitive to the requirement for rules of origin. The fact that a large number of firms prefer to trade with the United States over the MFN tariff rather than take advantage of duty-free NAFTA rules underlines the fact that firms find rules of origin both a cost and a nuisance.

A Common Approach to Non-Tariff Treatment of Third-Country Goods

While the tariff remains the largest item in establishing a common external trade policy, there are other aspects of how governments treat goods at the border that would need to be addressed as part of any deep integration arrangement. Nearly six decades of experience in applying GATT rules have added to the high level of convergence in the approach Canada and the United States take to the treatment of imported goods. The CUFTA and NAFTA added further precision to these rules and deepened convergence. Other than the items discussed below (agriculture, sanctions, trade remedies and government procurement), the universe of difference in the treatment of goods imported from third countries that would need to be tackled is relatively modest. Much border administration is more a matter of administrative convenience than of regulatory need. Most can be addressed on the basis of behind-the-border administrative and reporting requirements rather than on the basis of harmonized customs procedures. For example, labelling requirements on imported consumer goods are not identical, and need not be if both countries take the necessary steps to ensure compliance by other means.

One of the most important non-tariff barriers is the treatment of prohibited and restricted goods. Both countries have long lists of those goods, many of them similar in intent but different in detail. Many of the restrictions applied to goods at the border are part of the controls used to administer a wide range of domestic policy measures relating to consumer safety and similar goals and form part of the need to consider ways and means to overcome small but important differences in regulatory regimes.[50]

Sectoral Issues

While the border treatment of goods is largely a matter of developing horizontal rules, some specific sectoral issues will also need to be addressed, particularly in agriculture and, perhaps, energy. The differences between Canadian and US agricultural policies prompted Canada to insist that it be treated separately in the FTA and NAFTA. This may not be possible in a deeper integration arrangement, in part because over the past 20 years the agricultural aspects of cross-border trade and production patterns have also become more integrated. The trials and tribulations of the beef sector over the summer of 2003 demonstrated clearly the impact of deepening integration and the need for even greater regulatory co-operation.

There are three main areas of contention: US subsidy programs are larger than their Canadian equivalents; Canada's sensitive supply-managed sectors (dairy and poultry) would need to adjust to strong US competition while equivalent US sensitive sectors (peanuts, tobacco, cotton, wool and sugar) would not be much affected by competition from Canada; and the Canadian Wheat Board's state-trading practices in third markets continue to stick in the craw of a small coterie of US producers. None of these is easily resolved. Given the declining political clout of agricultural interests on both sides of the border, however, the time may have come for some serious effort to unblock barriers to a more sensible regime for agriculture, as was done, for example, for alcoholic beverages during the FTA, to the mutual benefit of both the industry and consumers.

There are some other technical issues unique to agriculture that would also need to be addressed, including food safety (on which there is already a high level of co-operation), rules governing consignment shipping and similar details of the distribution systems and weights and measures. None of these, however, pose insuperable obstacles, and all would bring significant benefits from higher levels of convergence and co-operation.

The North American energy market, and particularly the Canada-US energy market, is already substantially integrated with cross-border flows of energy in both directions. Canada is the leading foreign supplier of oil and gas to the US market, an important source of uranium, and an integral part of various electricity grids. Some regulatory hurdles remain, particularly in electricity, but they are not substantial impediments to cross-border trade. Canada's energy potential is an important element in US thinking about its national security and energy strategy, and security of supply considerations and prospects for future development by US interests are high.

Infrastructure development is the largest impediment to deeper integration in continental energy markets. The capacity to use energy as part of a strategic bargain in the broader context of a deep integration agreement, however, may be limited due to existing high levels of foreign investment and participation in Canada's energy sector, the absence of major problems in cross-border trade, limited supply, and provincial control over resource exploitation. Nevertheless, while the scope for trading off security of supply for concessions by the United States in other areas may be modest, the constructive psychological impact of an energy pact may be broader.

Agreed Ways of Dealing with Noncommercial Restrictions on Third-Party Trade

The United States has a long history of regarding trade sanctions as a useful tool of foreign policy. As the world's only hyperpower and hyperdemocracy, the call for trade and investment sanctions is often heard in Washington, and at times deployed, with or without the support of other nations. Canada, on the other hand, has traditionally been less willing to use trade sanctions as a tool for achieving nontrade objectives, and then only on the basis of broad international support through the United Nations, the Commonwealth or NATO.

Canadian critics assume that deeper integration would force Canada to align its foreign policy with that of the United States. The reality, however, is more subtle. The American resort to unilateral sanctions is rarer than is often realized.[51] While the call for sanctions may be more widespread in the United States, growing recognition of their limited impact and success has had a dampening effect on their deployment.[52] With the exception of Cuba, recent American sanctions tend to be shared by others, often including Canada. Additionally, modern information-sharing and reporting technologies make it possible to design ways and means to limit the commercial application of sanctions to the market of one of the partners.

An Agreed Approach to Trade Remedies

A more difficult issue arises from the application of trade remedies (antidumping and countervailing duties and emergency safeguards), either on third-party trade or on bilateral trade. Canada was the first country to apply an antidumping duty, but the United States has since become one of the most enthusiastic users of trade remedies, based on the deeply held conviction that foreigners are not always "fair." Canada learned during CUFTA negotiations how committed the United States is to the continued availability of trade remedies, and experience since then has not dulled this lesson.[53]

Nevertheless, the number of active trade remedy cases between Canada and the United States has steadily waned over the past 15 years, largely as a result of the impact of deeper integration, as well as the disciplinary impact of CUFTA/NAFTA chapter 19. Additionally, the rules of CUFTA/NAFTA have already largely eliminated access to safeguards on bilateral trade. The trade remedies issue, therefore, now revolves around antidumping and countervailing duties.

In the context of a deep integration arrangement, the two governments can make a virtue of the emerging reality of few cases and explore three strategies to further reduce the impact of trade remedies on internal trade: agree to eliminate access to cross-border trade to selected trade remedies in sectors that have had no new cases and where the preponderance of industry on both sides of the border agrees; work out ways to apply remedies to third-country imports on a joint basis for sectors thus exempted; and negotiate rules about resource pricing that will reduce the friction that has given rise to the most persistent and difficult cases. Given the increasing depth and extent of cross-border integration, making the transition from two separate to a single trade remedy regime makes commercial sense. Doing so on a gradual, sector-by-sector basis makes political sense.

During the transition period, the two countries would need to deploy techniques to ensure that trade remedy orders that apply to imports from one country are not evaded by importing through the other market. End-user certificates, for example, can be required on imports of goods entering the open market at a time when a trade remedy order is in place in the other. Again, the availability of sophisticated information-processing technologies makes such a strategy realistic today.

Access to Government Procurement Markets

It is for consideration whether a new round of negotiations offers a further opportunity to reduce the scope for discrimination in government procurement. From an economic welfare point of view, both countries would benefit from open and fully competitive government procurement markets at both the federal and at the state and provincial levels. With limited exceptions, this is a view that industry would share. Again, the increasingly integrated nature of production in North America makes the distinction between a Canadian and an American product more and more artificial and, probably, difficult to prove. The political economy of open procurement markets, however, is considerably more complicated, particularly in the United States and beneath the federal level. As a result, the two federal governments may wish to pursue a strategy that gradually opens government markets to full North American competition on a sectoral basis, reflecting the support of the preponderance of industry on both sides of the border.

Regulatory Convergence

The cross-border movement of goods could be substantially facilitated by eliminating the final vestiges of maintaining two separate customs territories. Much more will be achieved, however, as a result of a concerted program aimed at deepening regulatory convergence and eliminating minor regulatory differences that, as a matter of convenience, are often administered at the border.

Despite rhetorical commitments to freer trade, deregulation and privatization, markets continue to be governed by a detailed and dynamic framework of rules and regulations.[54] OECD governments, in particular, may have reduced their efforts to effect specific economic outcomes, but they have increased their roles in addressing risk and enhancing the quality of life. Rising living standards have increased demand for such social priorities as higher levels of health, safety, reliability, environmental protection, human rights and access to information, all of which rely on regulations.[55] Like earlier economic regulation, much of this regulatory activity can have profound effects on international trade and investment, underlining the need for co-operative approaches aimed at reducing the trade-distorting impact of differential regulation.

Within the Canada-US context, there already exists a high level of regulatory convergence, at least at the level of goals and objectives. The differences that do exist are more matters of detail and implementation, rather than of fundamental design.[56] Nevertheless, these differences impose costs and affect investment decisions. Much, therefore, can be gained by exploring ways and means by which such differences can be bridged or their impact ameliorated. The higher level of co-operation signalled by a deep integration arrangement provides an enhanced basis for pursuing various convergence strategies, including mutual recognition, co-operative enforcement, uniform product and process standards, the "tested-once" principle and even harmonization. The extent of regulations in both countries at all levels of jurisdiction suggests that this is a task that would need to be broken down along sectoral and functional lines and to include procedural and institutional capacity to address the dynamic character of most regulatory regimes.

Because of the interconnected nature of the Canadian and American economies, Canadian and American officials work together to manage and implement a vast array of similar, but not identical, regulatory regimes, from food safety to refugee determination.[57] The Centre for Trade Policy and Law has over the past year developed an extensive database detailing the extent of co-operation in 10 sectors, including customs administration, energy, agriculture and agri-food, surface transportation, immigration, drug approval, medical devices, chemicals and petrochemicals, environment, and financial services. In each case, the evidence indicates that officials have developed a dense network of informal co-operative arrangements to share information, experience, data and expertise with a view to improving regulatory outcomes, reducing costs, solving cross-border problems, implementing mutual recognition arrangements, establishing joint testing protocols and more. On any given day, dozens of American and Canadian officials at the federal, provincial and state levels work together, visiting, meeting, exchanging e-mails, taking phone calls and more. Virtually all of this activity takes place below the political radar screen. Little of it is co-ordinated or subject to a coherent, overall view of priorities or strategic goals. Some of it is mandated by formal agreements such as NAFTA or less formal memoranda of understanding. More importantly, much of this activity is the natural result of officials with similar responsibilities and shared outlooks seeking support and relationships to pursue them. This activity also reinforces, subtly and indirectly, the deepening integration of the two economies. In North America, unlike in Europe, integration has been largely "silent," that is, flowing from market forces and proximity rather than from government direction. NAFTA and similar arrangements mark efforts by governments to catch up with these forces of silent integration and provide appropriate and facilitating governance.

This paper is not the place to examine the full range of opportunities for regulatory co-operation, except to repeat that the negotiation of a deep integration agreement should provide an enhanced framework within which to explore and pursue such opportunities. Failure to do so would frustrate the attainment of the full benefits available from deepening integration.

The Cross-Border Movement of People

In negotiating the Canada-US FTA, Canada and the United States recognized that easing restrictions on the temporary entry of business travellers was critical to the success of the agreement. Not surprisingly, the chapters on temporary entry in both

CUFTA and the NAFTA have proven of immense value. It is for consideration, therefore, whether in negotiating a deep integration agreement, the two governments would want to take further steps to ease the cross-border movement of people. From an economic efficiency perspective, there is much to be gained from such steps. As technology has become more sophisticated and integration has deepened, the scope for delivering services on a cross-border basis has increased, and the key to service delivery is people. Similarly, as goods production has become more integrated along north-south lines, the need to deploy key personnel where they are most needed has increased. Thus, as helpful as the temporary entry provisions of FTA/NAFTA have proven, there is scope to do more. Doing more, however, engages security considerations, particularly in the aftermath of 9/11. Security threats are now much more varied and sophisticated than they were, and entry controls are critical to reducing risks. Addressing this as part of a broader effort at co-operation in addressing the treatment of people from third countries would significantly enhance the prospect of success and, concurrently, build confidence in the commitment of the two governments to the security of North America.

Administration of the Border

One of the most pressing issues facing the two governments is the high cost of administering the physical border, both for the two governments as well as for firms and individuals that use the border frequently to conduct their affairs in the integrated North American economy. A recent study suggests the costs may be as high as US$10 billion a year, or at least 2.7 percent of the total volume of trade.[58] Establishing a common commercial policy, reducing border barriers and eliminating most restrictions on the movement of people would not necessarily end border administration, but would simplify and reduce its extent — rules-of-origin certification, for example, would no longer be required.

In addition to routine customs and immigration activities, both Canada and the United States use border controls to interdict illegal immigration, drugs, terrorism and other criminal activities. Experience, however, suggests that the cost of border administration to pursue these goals is out of proportion to the results.[59] The border is simply too long and too porous to prevent determined cross-border criminal activity. Devoting even more customs and immigration resources at the bilateral border seems unlikely to achieve additional results, absent extraordinary additional investments in human and physical infrastructure. Increasing resources to such an extent, however, risks causing considerable collateral damage to economic interests in an effort to find solutions to a problem that can be handled more effectively and efficiently through other initiatives.

To that end, the two governments need to find ways to reduce the impact of the border by, for example, strengthening institutional contacts, enhancing co-operation, and sharing information on matters small and large. They need to explore investing further in intelligence gathering and gradually focusing ever larger parts of that effort on initial entries into North America. They could also make greater investments in infrastructure and in technology (both at ports-of-entry and in the corridors leading to such ports). Both types of investments are critical components of any comprehensive effort at improving the management of the border and reducing its commercial impact. Such investments need not proceed on the basis of current inspection methodologies, but should rely much more on risk assessments and random inspections.[60] They could also focus more on targeting resources toward pre-clearance programs for goods, vehicles and people. Finally, the two governments could enhance discussions about increasing the level of convergence in American and Canadian policies governing such matters as cargo and passenger pre-clearance programs, law enforcement programs of all types, and immigration and refugee determination procedures.

Efforts to make the border more effective and efficient are integral to the current Smart Border Accord. These discussions are proceeding at a snail's pace, because they are limited both by the decision to work within the confines of existing legislative mandates and by the lack of a strategic framework. Furthermore, they assume a continued need for current levels of border administration and thus are not aimed at eliminating or limiting the impact of the border, but at making that impact more efficient. Adding this effort to a broader commitment to negotiate a deep integration agreement would provide officials working on this file with the strategic vision they need to move beyond existing legislative mandates and provide them with greater scope to make useful trade-offs among competing priorities. The objective should be to create a border that is considerably more open and less bureaucratic, within a North America that is more secure. If Canadians and Americans want a smarter and less intrusive border, they will need to co-operate to create a more secure perimeter. The result should be a more open, more prosperous and more secure continent.

Institutional Arrangements

To manage and co-ordinate the more ambitious features of a deep integration agreement, Canada and the United States will need to establish the necessary institutional structures to provide for continuous adaptation to the governance demands of a dynamic and deeply integrated North American economy. In the words of a former senior official with extensive Canada-US experience, "What we have now is an institutional framework that is only half-evolved and that is straining to become something more, something greater, more comprehensive, more effective, with some in-built capacity for self-adjustment" (Legault 2002).

To offset the negative, unintended impact of difference and not hinder or impede desirable integration and increased market efficiencies, governments need to co-operate and co-ordinate their decisions more. The traditional approach focused on negotiating rules aimed at providing a framework within which governments pursued their regulatory responsibilities. In the face of deepening integration, such an approach is no longer sufficient. Instead, any new framework of rules needs to be supplemented by institutions and procedures geared to achieving a much higher level of co-operation, co-ordination, and even joint decision-making.[61]

Much of this co-ordination activity could involve existing institutions or invest officials in agencies on both sides of the border with new responsibilities. There is no reason, for example, why a new accord could not require Transport Canada and the American Department of Transportation to co-ordinate their efforts to ensure highway safety; before enacting any new rules and regulations, for example, mandatory co-ordination efforts would focus on ensuring compatible outcomes and mutual recognition of each other's approaches to the same problem. A good basis for this kind of co-operation already exists in the informal networks among officials and the relatively minor differences in regulatory approach. What is missing is an agreed mandate to resolve differences and a more formal institutional framework with authority to ensure mutually beneficial outcomes.

Similarly, both governments maintain separate but similar drug approval procedures that reach virtually identical conclusions, albeit within different time frames. Adapting these existing procedures to operate to the benefit of both countries could involve a commitment to more sharing and mutual recognition strategies and reducing duplication and overlap, while maintaining the capacity to address unique circumstances that may arise in one country or the other. Adopting a first-to-approve rule as a default position, for example, would lead to constructive regulatory competition, particularly if it includes a safeguard provision for sensitive issues. Establishing an international joint commission or similar institution to supervise the transition to a more integrated regime and provide continuing oversight thereafter would ensure that both governments maintain a voice in the drug approval process.

Canada and the United States have a long history of co-operation on environmental issues. More than 30 intergovernmental agreements on the environment have been reached between the two countries, beginning in 1909 with the Boundary Waters Treaty, which established the International Joint Commission (IJC). While many bilateral initiatives maintain an advisory and regulatory role, the IJC is an excellent example of a bilateral agency with the power to develop and implement regulations, manage shared resources and provide dispute-settlement procedures. It has played a particularly important role in the cleanup of the Great Lakes waters and region since the 1970s. Through the Canada-US Air Quality Agreement, the countries have been successful in regulating and reducing the pollutants that cause acid rain, leading to reductions in acid rain in the 1990s. The general ideology and science behind environmental policy in both countries is very similar, permitting relevant government agencies in both countries to collaborate closely to address transboundary environmental issues.

Beyond bilateral arrangements, both countries belong to numerous international environmental organizations and treaties. The Commission for Environmental Co-operation of North America (CEC) provides a forum for Canada, the United States and Mexico to manage shared environmental issues and to monitor and regulate the impact of trade on the environment.

Canada's ratification of the Kyoto Protocol has been identified as a potential stumbling block to co-operation on climate change issues, since the United States has refused to become a party to the protocol. Despite this, both countries have common approaches to addressing climate change, and even without ratification in the United States, efforts to reduce emissions are being undertaken. In 2002, Canada and the United States signed a Joint Agreement to Fight Climate Change, with the objective of expanding and intensifying bilateral efforts to address climate change.

Food safety is another area already invested with a high degree of co-operation. The Canadian Food Inspection Agency and Health Canada and the US Animal and Plant Health Inspection Service, Food Safety Inspection Service and Food and Drug Administration work closely together on the basis of hundreds of agreed protocols and understandings. Much of this co-operative activity, however, lacks the status of domestic law or the backing of international treaties, and any problems need to be resolved at the level of the minister and secretary of agriculture. Enshrining current levels of co-operation in a bilateral treaty and assigning supervisory responsibility for the continued adaptation of its implementation to a new, bilateral institution would greatly enhance consumer and producer confidence in the two governments' commitment to governing what is, *de facto,* an integrated market for food products.

More generally, the Canada-United States Agriculture "Record of Understanding Agreement" (ROU), signed in 1998, provides another model of co-operation. Its stated objective is to promote more open and fair trade in agricultural products between Canada and the United States. The ROU requires the Canadian minister and the US secretary of agriculture to meet "at least" annually to review the state of bilateral trade. Sub-Cabinet level officials are required to meet at least twice per year. The formal consultative mechanisms of the ROU are the Canada-United States Consultative Committee on Agriculture (CCA) and the Province-State Advisory Group (PSAG).

The CCA provides a high-level forum to strengthen bilateral agriculture trade relations between Canada and the United States through co-operation and co-ordination and facilitates discussion and co-operation on matters related to agriculture between the two countries. It serves as an early warning system by recognizing and addressing existing bilateral agricultural issues, as well as those that may arise in the future. The committee meets approximately twice per year. The CCA is led by senior officials from the US Department of Agriculture, the Office of the US Trade Representative, Agriculture and Agri-Food Canada, and the Department of Foreign Affairs and International Trade. Significant progress has been made in many of the critical areas of concern identified at its creation. The PSAG represents the agricultural interests of producers at the state and provincial level. The PSAG has no responsibility to negotiate on bilateral issues, but reports to the CCA and provides industry and public stakeholders – through their provincial and state governments – a forum to discuss agricultural concerns.

These various initiatives in the agriculture and agri-food sector suggest a high level of trust and co-operation between officials and a solid foundation on which to build more formal mechanisms for further co-operation, joint decision-making and problem-solving.

Through the Shared Border Accord, Citizenship and Immigration Canada, the Department of Foreign Affairs and International Trade, Canada Customs and Revenue Agency, the US Immigration and Naturalization Service (USINS), US Customs, and the US State Department agreed to work together toward four main goals: enhance protection against illegal and irregular border activity; facilitate movement of goods; promote international trade; and reduce costs by increasing efficiencies. Through the Border Vision Process, USINS and Citizenship and Immigration Canada agreed to develop a joint regional approach to migration though information- and intelligence-sharing, policy co-ordination, joint overseas operations, and border co-operation. Again, the foundation for more formal co-operation and joint decision-making exists, but the institutional structure required to take it to the next level will need to be developed in order to invest bilateral joint decision-making with the required political oversight.

In sector after sector, these networks of co-operation ensure a high level of normal, day-to-day co-ordination. They also promote, directly and indirectly, convergence in how the two governments regulate the myriad of quality-of-life and economic regulations. The database being developed at CTPL illustrates that co-operation among officials is ubiquitous, taking many forms. The challenge is to channel much of this existing activity and make it work more effectively in providing better governance of the Canada-US economy. In some areas, more formal and independent co-ordination mechanisms might be required, in some areas on a permanent basis, in others as transitional measures. As negotiations proceed in establishing a new Canada-US deep integration agreement, negotiators would identify areas where it would be appropriate to establish bilateral joint commissions or analogous institutions charged with co-ordinating and supervising the regulatory activities of the two governments, and to address any conflict arising out of the regulatory activities of the states and provinces as well as the two federal governments.

Establishment of such joint commissions could be phased in over time as progress is made in implementing the new commitments and as confidence develops in the efficacy of such joint decision-making. As with the existing International Joint Commission, ultimate political authority would continue to rest with the two governments, but by appointing high-quality commissioners and pledging to maintain an arm's-length relationship with each commission, the two governments would seek to foster a similar, respected status for the new commissions.[62]

Issues for Further Research

THE ABOVE ANALYSIS SUGGESTS THAT THE KEYS TO A SUCCESSFUL BILATERAL INITIATIVE to modernize the governance of deepening integration lie in finding better ways to effect co-operative approaches to regulatory issues which, in turn, will depend on innovative ways to build institutional capacity for information-sharing and joint decision-making. The most important impact of the successful pursuit of these twin tasks will be felt at the border. It will result in a much more open and less intrusive border as part of a North American society that is both more cohesive and secure and capable of protecting the capacity of each government to express the democratic will of the governed. In thinking these issues through, three important areas suggest themselves for further, policy-oriented research.

First, a thorough assessment comparing what is done at the border now and what would be required at the border as a result of the development of more formal institutions and networks of co-operation backing up a much higher level of regulatory co-operation is required. We need a better grasp of the issues now addressed at the border that (1) would no longer need to be done at all; (2) could be done more efficiently and effectively by other means; and (3) must continue to be done regardless of the level of co-operation and trust.

Second, we need a detailed, sector-by-sector survey of current levels of regulatory co-operation and similarity and an assessment of the scope for doing more, including work on political and economic costs and benefits.

Third, a systemic examination of institutional designs capable of balancing the desirability of greater convergence and co-operation and the need to maintain scope for democratic accountability and political oversight should be conducted.

Concluding Observations

CANADA AND THE UNITED STATES FACE AN HISTORIC CHALLENGE: DO THEY CONTINUE on the path of co-operation in promoting more secure and more prosperous North American societies or do they pursue divergent and, ultimately, less secure and less prosperous courses? To ask the question is to answer it, and yet, if important decisions are not taken soon, the two countries may well find themselves on divergent paths. Such a development would be a tragic mistake, a mistake that can be readily avoided if the two governments commit to a series of deliberate and co-operative steps that will enhance both the security and the prosperity of their citizens.

Working together, of course, is not a new experience. Ever since President Franklin D. Roosevelt and Prime Minister Mackenzie King crafted the first Good Neighbour trade agreement in 1935 and the Ogdensburg Declaration on defence in 1940, the two governments have seen their mutual physical security and economic well-being as inextricably linked. Over the course of the subsequent seven decades, political leaders and public servants have crafted hundreds of agreements, arrangements, institutions and networks based on the fundamental premise that working together will pay huge dividends, while working at cross purposes will lead to loss and failure on both sides of the border.

Canadians and Americans must now come to grips with the fact that their extensive network of trade and security arrangements has worked exceedingly well, but that it no longer addresses directly the needs and circumstances in which the two countries now find themselves. In the words of *Globe and Mail* columnist Drew Fagan, "the solution for both countries is a new kind of arrangement that goes far beyond NAFTA: mixing the economic security Canada needs with the physical security Americans demand" (2003). Ironically, these two seemingly divergent priorities are, in fact, convergent: success in one will strengthen the other and vice versa; confidence in security arrangements is critical to underpinning economic well-being, and economic growth is critical to strengthening security arrangements. The end result should be two societies working closely together to keep terrorist and other enemy forces from North America's shores, promote democracy and freedom around the world, strengthen prosperity at home and abroad and improve the quality of life on both sides of the border.

To get there, the two countries need to face up to a number of realities. First, they already share a perimeter. It is defined by geography, economics, demographics, shared political and societal values, common security arrangements and challenges, and joint economic arrangements and goals. The issue today is how, in the face of terrorist threats and economic opportunities, the two countries can strengthen the perimeter that already exists and make it work more effectively to their mutual benefit.

Second, broad convergence already exists across a wide range of public policy areas, including security and immigration. The differences that do exist lie in administration, not in fundamental concept. While people in either country may at times want to celebrate the differences, all need also to recognize the many similarities, common values and shared goals. The need is not for harmonization, but for more sharing of information, co-operation and co-ordination, both within each country and between them. What counts is that the two governments share objectives and have confidence in outcomes.

Finally, deepening integration will continue between the two countries across virtually every area where the two societies connect. The question for the two governments is whether to help or hinder that integration, manage it or let it drift. In the words of former Canadian ambassador to the United States, Allan Gotlieb, "Canada should look to a broader, and deeper economic and security zone in which the rules of engagement would be less arbitrary, more predictable and provide greater common security" (2002a).

Any initiative needs to be comprehensive in scope and its results need to be enshrined in a formal agreement. Comprehensive initiatives ease the task of building the necessary broad base of support required to overcome highly focused opposition groups and reluctant bureaucratic agendas. The exigencies of the highly fragmented US political system also make it very difficult for US officials to accommodate foreign interests on an issue-by-issue basis, while the capacity to exercise raw power makes it relatively easy to insist that foreign governments accommodate single-issue US interests. Broad agendas and formal agreements help to reduce this disparity in power.

The challenge for Canadians and Americans is to exercise, rather than guard, their sovereignty by anticipating change and preparing options that promote each other's interests. For Canadians, a "smart" future lies not in imitating what Americans do, but in astutely leveraging the advantages of proximity to the world's leading and largest economy. The options are clear. Canada and the United States need to take deliberate steps to bring the architecture of their relationship into line with the challenge and fact of deepening interdependence as well as with the political and security realities ushered in by the events of 9/11.

Notes

Much of the analysis in this paper was originally prepared as a contribution to the *North American Security and Prosperity Initiative* of the Canadian Council of Chief Executives (CCCE). I am grateful to Thomas d'Aquino, president and chief executive officer of the CCCE, for kind permission to use this material. The analysis has also benefited from the research initiatives of the Centre for Trade Policy and Law on institutional and regulatory issues affecting Canada-United States trade relations, sponsored in part by the Department of Foreign Affairs and Investment Partnerships Canada. The views expressed here are my own and do not necessarily reflect those of the CCCE or the federal government.

1 We concluded that "overwhelmingly, Canada's leading trade and foreign policy partner is the United States, surpassing all other partnerships combined in the breadth, depth, and intensity of the relationship. Cross-border trade and investment drive our economy. US innovation and entrepreneurship provide both opportunities and competition. US popular culture dominates, not because it is forced on Canadians but because Canadians choose it. The US military provides a blanket of security. US warm weather cossets millions of Canadians each winter. The US presence pervades every aspect of Canadian life, including, as Foreign Minister Bill Graham recognizes, foreign policy. Virtually every aspect of Canada's political, economic, cultural, and social life is measured by Canadians in terms of the US yardstick...The first and only priority for Canadian diplomacy over the next few years is to reach a new accommodation with the United States...Canada and the United States should take deliberate steps to bring the architecture of their relationship into line with the challenge and fact of deepening integration, as well as with the political and security realities ushered in by the events of September 11" (Dymond and Hart 2003).

2 A broader assessment of public attitudes to international trade and trade agreements can be found in Mendelsohn and Wolfe (2000).

3 Poll results accessed at www.sesresearch.com

4 Greenspon and Bricker provide a more detailed analysis of this perspective (2001).

5 While the national mood points to a willingness to consider steps toward facilitating deeper integration, it does not suggest either an appetite for, or a concern with, the development of North American citizenship to bolster the legitimacy of deepening integration. Academic analysts find such issues fascinating, as does Jennifer Welch in her paper, "Prospects and Pathways for North American Integration: The Implications for Citizenship" (2003) but most Canadians and their political leaders do not see such issues as pertinent to the problems and solutions under consideration. The European experience, as pointed out below, is also much less pertinent to North American circumstances than many academic analysts assert.

6 The discussion is captured in a subsequent article edited by Michael Hart (2000).

7 For example, the Shared Border Accord announced in 1995 and the Canada-US Partnership Forum formed in 1999, each with the professed claim of creating, in the words of former minister of national revenue, David Anderson, "a hassle-free border for honest travellers and businesses, and a brick wall for those who try to smuggle or break other laws at this border" (*New York Times,* 4 October 2001).

8 In October 2001, for example, the Conference Board of Canada released a special report, *Border Choices: Balancing the Need for Security and Trade*, calling on the government to eliminate border inspections together with the negotiation of a customs union. In November 2001, a newly formed business Coalition for Secure Trade and Efficient Borders called for "a comprehensive and integrated solution" to security and border issues. In December 2001, the Canadian Council of Chief Executives (CCCE) announced the creation of an Action Group on Canada-US Co-operation, co-chaired by former mandarins and now council members, Derek Burney and Paul Tellier. David Bradley, chief executive of the Canadian

Trucking Association, was one of the earliest and most articulate spokespersons for a major effort to redefine Canada-US trade relations, suggesting that "the current focus on border issues in both countries may well represent a rare window of opportunity to achieve progress on an integrated and more rational border processing system" (*National Post*, 15 October 2001).

9 In November 2001, for example, the Public Policy Forum convened a conference in Toronto on "Canada's Policy Choices: Managing Our Border with the United States." In September 2002, a coalition of policy groups, including the Institute for Research on Public Policy, organized the first of five planned conferences entitled "Borderlines: Canada's Options in North America." Critics of free trade and deepening Canada-US integration organized a conference on "Canada, Free Trade and Deep Integration in North America: Revitalizing Democracy, Upholding the Public Good" at York University in Toronto, 15-16 October 2003, in order to advance "a distinct vision of social and economic development than that proposed by corporate Canada." See http://www.yorku.ca/cerlac/deep-integration. html

10 A description of the initiative is available at www.ceocouncil.ca.

11 See, for example, articles in the *Fraser Forum* for March 2002 and March 2003.

12 The Public Policy Forum, under the direction of David Zussman, pursued a number of initiatives aimed at strengthening understanding of the implications of deepening Canada-US integration. See http://www.ppforum.com/gs/gs.htm

13 A more thoughtful version of this view can be found in a series of columns by David Crane in the *Toronto Star* (9, 13, and 16 August 2003). Canadian Labour Congress secretary-treasurer, Hassan Yussuff, also provides a complete catalogue of the nationalist view of free trade and deeper bilateral integration in a speech delivered at the 2003 Couchiching conference, "Sovereignty or Standard of Living" (2003).

14 Jackson insists the current focus on Canada-US border issues distracts attention from Canada's "real" problems: the failure of corporate Canada to innovate and to invest adequately in research and development, workers, skills, and new plants and equipment. As such, his view represents a typical expression of the nationalist lament about the retreat of the state and the embrace of market forces, developments now accepted by four of the five parties in the House of Commons, presumably because politicians sense that Canadians do not want to retreat from these policies.

15 Like Jackson, Campbell wants to "reassert and rebuild" the capacity of government as an active manager of the economy, rather than as a bystander to the "excesses and failures" of the market (15), by focusing on strengthening the national economy and national demand through a variety of macroeconomic, labour market and industrial policy tools. He wants to find ways to "prune back the most egregious aspects" of NAFTA (9), to strengthen social services and cultural exemptions, to eliminate the investor-state dispute mechanism and to revisit the "third option" to diversify trade, economic and cultural relationships with other nations (10, 2003).

16 Dobbin believes the government must seek out other partners in foreign policy initiatives to enhance and preserve the principles of multilateralism and internationalism.

17 It should be noted, however, that while results to date are minimal, activity is not. Various task forces, committees and initiatives throughout the government are seized by the need to gain a better appreciation of the challenges facing Canada-US relations, including co-ordinating work by the Policy Research Initiative and the Canadian Centre for Management Development. Little of this will emerge for public consumption until such time as a more welcoming political climate is perceived in Ottawa.

18 See the statement issued by the three NAFTA ministers (Pettigrew, Canales and Zoellick 2003). In subsequent comments to the press, Pettigrew assured them that Canada was not entering into customs union discussions. See also press reports for 8 October 2003.

19 Or, as former Canadian ambassador the United States, Derek Burney, put it in a recent speech: "Neglect of Canada is a chronic condition in America...that does little damage to US interests...and is not necessarily all that bad for us. The hard reality — and often the most difficult reality for us to stomach — is that the reverse is not the case. If we neglect the effort of engagement and avoid raising Canada's profile and concerns forcefully and consistently...we pay a disproportionate price" (2004, 46).

20 Some might include values, but as Denis Stairs points out, we need to be careful not to confuse values with interests. Canadian and American values may sometimes diverge, even if our interests do not. Our values are in many respects similar, even if they are sometimes expressed in different ways. By focusing on small nuances in values, we also sometimes fail to see the extent to which we share interests. See Stairs (2001, 2003). Bill Dymond and I explore the confusion inherent in values-based foreign policy in "The Potemkin Village of Canadian Foreign Policy."

21 The classic discussion of divergent Canadian and US values can be found in Seymour Martin Lipset (1989). The recent book by Michael Adams, with Amy Langstaff and David Jamieson suggests that a further 15 years of deepening economic integration has in no way undermined this divergence (2003). Indeed, if their polling and analysis is to be credited, divergence in popular values is deepening even as convergence in economic ties and policies is growing. This theme is explored in considerable detail in William Watson's book (1998), which demonstrates that Canadians remain free to choose what kind of government they want, regardless of the depth of economic integration and the adoption of integration-facilitating policies.

22 Canadian-born Harvard economist John Kenneth Galbraith captured this well during the CUFTA debate when he noted: "I was brought up in southwestern Ontario where we were taught that Canadian patriotism should not withstand anything more than a five-dollar wage differential. Anything more, and you went to Detroit" (1985).

23 Former Canadian diplomat Leonard Legault went on to say that "a wrong-headed notion of sovereignty can actually interfere with one of the most fundamental expressions of sovereignty — the pursuit of national interests" (2002).

24 What economists call liberalization, political scientists consider the retreat of the state. For many political analysts, the essence of Canadian nationhood is the result of policies that discriminated in favour of Canadians at the expense of foreigners, particularly Americans. Such nation-building policies, from railways to banking to communications, aimed at building a Canadian-owned, east-west economy. These policies, however, were gradually undermined by first the Canada-US Reciprocal Trade Agreement of 1935 and then the General Agreement on Tariffs and Trade (GATT), and were given a fatal blow by CUFTA and NAFTA. The result has been a massive reorientation of the Canadian economy from east-west to north-south, growing dependence on the US market and less reliance on government programs. Of course, missing from this analysis is the impact that the erosion of nation-building policies has had on the prosperity of most Canadians, explaining the lack of support among the vast majority of Canadians for a return to state-centric, nation-building policies. See John McDougall, "The Long-Run Determinants of Deep/Political Canada-US Integration," for a discussion of the role of nation-building policies in Canada's development, and the implications of their erosion over the past twenty years (2003).

25 Nancy Olewiler concludes, for example, "that the evidence...does not support the view that greater integration of the North American economies must result in lower levels of environmental quality... Regulations, if they have moved at all, appear to be converging to at least the status quo level of the country with the most stringent regulations. There appears to be a trend toward tightening regulations and a very slow creep toward the use of more

cost-effective market-based policies" (2003, 560). In a similar vein in the same volume, Gerard Boychuk and Keith Banting wryly conclude that for social programs, "a more pervasive pattern of convergence may be just around the corner. At a minimum, however, the corner seems to be getting further away" (2003, 560).

26 Brian Tomlin and Bruce Doern (1991) do a good job of debunking this cherished myth of foreign policy elites. Allan Gotlieb notes "Canada's greatest asset on the international stage is our relationship with the United States. Yet Canadian politicians and diplomats seem fixated on taking positions designed to differentiate us from our neighbour. While it is true that many Canadians worry about an apparent US willingness to act alone in the world, this does not mean we differ on fundamental values and purposes. The special relationship of trust, affinity and shared values that Canada built up with the United States over the years, provides us with an opportunity few others have to influence the world's most powerful actor and help shape its international positions. Wouldn't such an approach to our relationship be more prone to achieving results than publicly lecturing and hectoring? If we publicly support the world's greatest democracy, could anyone rationally believe this would compromise our independence?" (2002b).

27 See, for example, Wolfe (2003). A similar sentiment was expressed by Sylvia Ostry and Gilbert Winham (2003). At a more general but less informed level, former Foreign Minister Lloyd Axworthy continues to advance this view in, for example, his new book, *Navigating a New World* (2003). Allan Gotlieb subjected it to a searching review in the *National Post* (2003d), concluding that multilateral visions of a brave new world cannot be realized in the absence of the United States, a prospect that troubles Axworthy greatly.

28 The original six forged a special set of preferential relations with their former colonies in the 1960s. In the 1970s, after the UK and Denmark moved from the European Free Trade Association (EFTA) to the Common Market, the latter negotiated bilateral free trade agreements with the remaining members of EFTA. At the same time, association agreements were developed with various Mediterranean countries, a technique used later to build relationships with Eastern European members in waiting. More complex agreements were also concluded with the growing number of former colonies. The result has been a complex web of arrangements loosely blessed by the rules of the multilateral regime. The lesson is that governments do what they consider important and develop the necessary international legal cover later.

29 For some analysts, particularly those with legal training, NAFTA now constitutes the indispensable foundation from which all future bilateral or trilateral trade and investment negotiations must proceed. Perhaps, but it is also possible to view NAFTA as an agreement whose time came but is now largely gone. Between Canada and the United States, it is now fully implemented. Most of its provisions would be very difficult to undo. Its main continuing importance lies in the dispute-settlement provisions set out in chapters 11 and 19; even chapter 20 has been largely superseded by the WTO Dispute Settlement Understanding. I do not mean to suggest that we can now abrogate NAFTA, but rather that like those of the 1935 and 1938 Reciprocal Trade Agreements, the 1947 GATT, and the 1965 Autopact, NAFTA's objectives have been largely realized. Any successor agreement may need to incorporate some of its elements (e.g., chapters 11 and 19), but need not be trilateral. Should Canada and the United States proceed to an agreement that moves well beyond the contours of conventional trade agreements, the precedential value of NAFTA will be minimal.

30 In "A Trilateral Mirage: A Tale of Two Americas," a paper prepared for the Canadian Defence and Foreign Affairs Institute in June 2003, Jean Deaudelin of the Norman Paterson School of International Affairs at Carleton comes to a less accommodating conclusion: "Canada's bilateral relationship with the United States

is vital and its management should not be cluttered by the massive complexity of Mexico-US affairs...Canada's relations with Mexico...will remain marginal to the country's core interests." Hufbauer and Schott (2004), on the other hand, conclude that US political sensitivities make anything other than a trilateral initiative unrealistic. Discussions with US officials suggest that US political sensitivities are more nuanced, providing scope for differentiated approaches. The difficulties of a trilateral approach that considers both economic and security issues are also well illustrated by the paper prepared for conference, The Art of the State II, by Stéphane Roussel and Athanasios Hristoulas, "The Quest for trilateral security in North America."

31 Recent economic analysis has tried to unravel the extent to which these emerging patterns flow from the broad impact of globalization, the magnetic effect of a red-hot US economy, or the FTA/NAFTA. Such analysis, fascinating as it may be for economic modellers, poses questions to which there are at best speculative answers and that are of only marginal interest to current policy issues. The extent of integration is clear. It has been largely market driven, and policy has played a secondary, if important, facilitating role. This is not to denigrate policy, but to place it in context. Policy can continue to play an important facilitating role, but, except if there is a major redirection in policy, it is unlikely to change the basic direction of ever-deepening integration. A review of the literature assessing the economic impact of the FTA/NAFTA was presented to the IRPP conference "Art of the State II: Thinking North America: Prospects and Pathways," by John Curtis (2003).

32 Some analysts express concern that Canada is not getting an appropriate "share" of global FDI, and conclude that CUFTA/NAFTA did not have the predicted investment effect. Such analysts are looking at the wrong evidence. Free trade did have a major investment effect, evident, for example, in the massive reorientation of the Canadian economy from an east-west to a north-south axis. It also helped to dispose Canadian investors to direct more of their savings toward foreign opportunities: in 1997 Canada crossed an historic divide from a net importer of capital to a net exporter, a position suggesting the emergence of a more mature economy. Whatever Canada's appropriate "share" of global FDI, the past two decades have seen Canadians become steadily more involved in global capital markets, both as investors and as hosts of foreign investments, taking advantage of growing specialization, expertise and entrepreneurial confidence. For a detailed discussion of North American FDI flows, see Globerman (2003).

33 In his analysis, Cross emphasizes how industry has reorganized production to take advantage of a more open border. While the automotive sector has moved furthest along the integration spectrum, other sectors are not far behind, including machinery and equipment, electronics, plastics and textiles. Even resource industries, including metals and minerals and forest products, exhibit a surprising level of import content in their exports (2002, figure 2).

34 Industry Canada, in its North American Linkages project, has catalogued the wide range of linkages that form part of the emerging pattern of deepening cross-border integration. See Harris (2003). Fry also provides a useful catalogue of the extent of integration (2003).

35 The initial intellectual basis for differentiating between the various stages of integration was largely the work of economists. Subsequently, these categories also gained legal status as a result of their use in the GATT, and now the WTO, rules governing the creation of preferential or regional agreements. These rules, of course, were developed to protect the interests of non-members rather than to provide guidance on how to structure agreements that respond to the goals of participating governments in specific circumstances.

36 GATT Article XXIV provides that "A free-trade area shall be understood to mean a group of two or more customs territories in which the duties and other restrictive regulations of commerce (except, where neces-

sary, those permitted under Articles XI, XII, XIII, XIV, XV and XX) are eliminated on substantially all the trade between the constituent territories in products originating in such territories" (para 8b). The permissive articles are largely related to measures taken to regulate foreign exchange and to safeguard the balance of payments and issues related to permitted exceptions.

37 GATT Article XXIV provides that "A customs union shall be understood to mean the substitution of a single customs territory for two or more customs territories, so that (i) duties and other restrictive regulations of commerce (except, where necessary, those permitted under Articles XI, XII, XIII, XIV, XV and XX) are eliminated with respect to substantially all the trade between the constituent territories of the union or at least with respect to substantially all the trade in products originating in such territories, and, (ii) subject to the provisions of paragraph 9, substantially the same duties and other regulations of commerce are applied by each of the members of the union to the trade of territories not included in the union" (para 8a).

38 Monnet noted in one of the most quoted passages of his *Memoirs* that "there will be no peace in Europe if States reconstitute themselves on a basis of national sovereignty...European countries are too confined to ensure prosperity and essential social developments for their people. It follows that European States should form themselves into a federation or a 'European entity' which would make them a joint economic unit." Monnet was drawing on a long and distinguished intellectual tradition in Europe that equated peace and security with economic integration, exemplified by the influential book by Norman Angell (1978). Winston Churchill, drawing on the same intellectual tradition, wrote to his foreign secretary during the dark days of 1942: "I look forward to a United States of Europe in which the barriers between the nations will be greatly minimized and unrestricted travel will be possible" (Monnet and Churchill, quoted in Wistrich [1991, 24 and 23]).

39 The accession of Poland, the Czech Republic, Slovakia, Hungary, Slovenia, Lithuania, Estonia, Latvia, Malta and Cyprus in 2004 is predicated not only on enlarging the market and reducing barriers to trade and investment, but even more on reinforcing democracy and market-based reforms in these countries. All went through an extended accession negotiation assessing their capacity to implement the *acquis communautaires* and sustain democracy.

40 As John Dales has pointed out, in adopting the National Policy, Canadian politicians opted for a policy that emphasized aggregate growth rather than productivity, efficiency and competitiveness. In that, they succeeded. In the century that followed, Canada's population grew by a factor of six and its economy by a factor of at least 50, but this was at the expense of the individual prosperity of Canadians. See Dales (1966).

41 It is important here to distinguish between border effects that are amenable to policy change and those that are not. As the work of John McCallum and John Helliwell (1994) suggests, the impact of institutional, geographic and similar barriers can have important impacts on trade and investment patterns. By comparing trade between provinces and between states and provinces of comparable size and geographic separation, they estimated that the border effect was in the order of 17 in 1988; that is, the propensity for trade between Canadian provinces was 17 times higher than that for trade between the provinces and states of equal size and distance. While one may quarrel about some of their assumptions, the quality of the evidence on which they relied, or the methodology of the study, they made a provocative case that borders continue to have an important effect on trade, investment and distribution patterns. In a later study, Helliwell (1998, 115) estimated that CUFTA had reduced this border effect to a factor of 12 by 1996, but that there was little prospect for further reduction. I disagree. Policy and market forces can, over time, reduce these impacts. The elimination and reduction of overt forms of

discrimination, such as tariffs and quotas, will have immediate, measurable effects. Institutional barriers may also be affected by policy changes, however. For example, the gradual development of secure channels of supply and high levels of trust will, over time, have a subtle but important impact on trade and investment patterns. It should be noted that Helliwell's enthusiasm for the benefits of liberalization and openness is considerably less than that of most economists, as demonstrated in Helliwell (2002).

42 For example, Bill Dymond and I analyze the role of ownership restrictions in meeting Canadian cultural policy objectives and conclude that "there is no necessary connection between the nationality of investors and the government's capacity to regulate their activity to satisfy public policy objectives.... Whatever their line of business, private firms exist to return a profit to their owners. There is no appreciable difference between the profit-maximizing interests of a privately owned bank, automotive manufacturing facility, film production company or publishing enterprise. There is also no discernible difference between the profit-maximizing interests of an American, German or Canadian bank or publishing enterprise. And there is no difference in the capacity of governments to regulate any of these enterprises, regardless of the nationality of their owners. Any firm pursuing its profit-maximizing interests in the Canadian market is subject to the laws of Canada" (Dymond and Hart 2001a).

43 Current policy squabbling about the cross-border sales of Canadian-based Internet pharmacies have less to do with drug safety than with the reluctance of multinational pharmaceutical firms to enforce their patent rights in Canada (Internet pharmacies are selling outside the territory for which they are licensed), ostensibly for public relations reasons. Similarly, provincial pharmacy licensing boards and medical associations seem unwilling to discipline their members for selling outside their territory or for signing prescriptions for patients they have never seen. All three may regret their short-sightedness as governments look to more heavy-handed solutions. The issue, however, should not obscure the high level of convergence in the two countries' intellectual property regimes.

44 Over the last two years, US prosecution of the war on terrorism and against Iraq appears to have raised the antipathy of many Canadians. Much of this seems more focused on President Bush than on the United States as a country. Increasingly, Canadians feel more comfortable with Democratic than Republican politicians. Ironically, Canadian needs and desires in a deep integration agreement and a new accommodation with the United States are more likely to appeal to a Republican than a Democratic administration. Once again, Canadians seem to be confusing sentiment and interest in their approach to the United States.

45 The simple average of all applied MFN tariff rates for Canada is 6.8 percent, while that for the United States is 5.5 percent. Of course, within these simple averages lies a wide dispersion of rates, including astronomical rates for selected agricultural products, such as 350 percent for tobacco in the United States and 238 percent for cheese in Canada. See Goldfarb for a breakdown of these averages by broad categories (2003, table 3). Goldfarb provides tables that set out comparative rates for various sectors and groups of products and identifies where some of the more sensitive tariff peaks can be found (e.g., ships and supply-managed agricultural products for Canada, tobacco, peanuts, footwear and textiles and clothing for the United States).

46 The Senate Foreign Affairs Committee's rejection of a customs union on the grounds that it would require unacceptable "sacrifices" of Canadian sovereignty, largely related to the setting of tariff rates on third-country trade, is difficult to take seriously. As the analysis that follows indicates, the tariff is a waning policy instrument, with little left that would warrant such a conclusion. It also ignores a consistent theme in Canadian trade policy: eliminate the application of tariffs on as much Canadian trade as possible, and use the Canadian tariff

as "payment." A customs union can be effectively deployed to achieve much of this longstanding goal (see Senate 2003, 67-69).

47 WTO rules require that any averaging exercise result in a CET that is, on average, no more protective than the protective effect of the two separate tariffs. By taking, as a point of departure, application of the lower of the two rates for most tariffs, the two governments would leave themselves wide discretion to address the relatively modest list of difficult cases.

48 Both countries also apply the GPT to imports from so-called "transitional" economies, that is, former central planning economies, many of them successor states that emerged from the former Soviet Union.

49 Canada has FTAs with Israel, Mexico, Chile, Costa Rica, and is negotiating with the remaining EFTA countries, Singapore, and Central America (El Salvador, Guatemala, Honduras, and Nicaragua). The United States has FTAs with Israel, Mexico, Chile and Jordan; is negotiating FTAs with Australia, Singapore, Central America (Costa Rica, El Salvador, Guatemala, Honduras, and Nicaragua), and Morocco; and is considering FTAs with South Africa, Bahrain and other Middle Eastern partners. Canada also has special rates in effect for Australia and New Zealand (the last remnants of the old British preferential tariff), and for Commonwealth Caribbean countries. The United States has special tariff rates for the Caribbean Basin countries (except Cuba) and those benefiting from the *Africa Growth and Opportunity Act* and the *Andean Preference Act*. It is worth adding that Mexico has concluded a much larger and more complex web of preferential arrangements. Adding Mexico to a North American customs union would require that Mexico be prepared to come to terms with this complicating factor.

50 The more significant discrepancies tend to arise in the laws that the two customs services enforce on behalf of other governmental agencies. Consequently, they are part of the regulatory differences within various other sectors and not Customs issues, per se. US Customs enforces import and export permits on alcoholic beverages, animals and animal products, certain drugs, firearms and ammunition, fruits, nuts, meat and meat products, plants and plant products; poultry and poultry products, petroleum and petroleum products, vegetables, viruses, serums and toxins; it enforces certification requirements on imports of tobacco, plant seeds, eggs, viruses, serums, toxins and antitoxins; and ensures compliance with regulations of other agencies for art materials, cultural property, hazardous/toxic/flammable materials, household appliances, some electronics products, toys and children's articles, various trademarked and copyrighted products, and textiles and clothing. Canadian customs enforces export and import permit requirements on dairy products, poultry, toxic substances, wheat and wheat products, controlled drugs and substances, weapons, firearms and ammunition, cultural property, oil, gas and electricity, explosives, beef and veal products, plant and animal specimens or products, steel, softwood lumber, certain types of fish, and nuclear energy; it also enforces certification requirements on imports of pest control products, radio-communication equipment, and imports and exports of wild plants and animals.

51 Currently, United States trade sanctions generally prohibit trade with Cuba, Iran, Iraq, Libya, North Korea, Serbia and Sudan. Additionally, persons designated as having promoted the proliferation of weapons of mass destruction, named foreign terrorist organizations, designated terrorists and narcotics traffickers, and the Taliban face restrictions on imports into the US. Vessels and aircraft under the registry, control or ownership of sanctions targets cannot import merchandise into the United States. Cuban cigars and Iranian carpets can only be imported under certain restrictions. Finally, diamonds from Angola must be accompanied by a certificate verifying that they are not "conflict diamonds." Canada currently sanctions trade with Myanmar and Angola; controls the export of firearms, weapons and devices listed in the Export Control List to countries with which Canada has an inter-

governmental defence, research, development and production arrangements; and maintains some controls on exports to Iraq, North Korea, Cuba, Libya, Iran, Bolivia.

52 Gary Hufbauer and his colleagues at the Institute for International Economics have made extensive studies of the intended and corollary effects of sanctions and conclude that they rarely meet their stated objective and usually cause a good deal of collateral harm (see Elliott et al. 2004).

53 It is important to add that the highest level of enthusiasm resides in what some analysts have called the "iron triangle" of administrators, legislative assistants and lawyers, all of whom have a vested interest in an active trade remedy regime. The interest of administrators and the trade bar is not difficult to divine; the role of legislative assistants becomes clearer when it is appreciated that many of them aspire to become lobbyists or administrators, and if they are lawyers, members of the trade bar. The enthusiasm on the part of business in the United States for trade remedies has become more muted over the years and is largely confined to a few sectors that have become the mainstay of the system, with steel at the forefront.

54 The effective operation of the market is critically dependent on the existence of a supporting framework of rules, regulations and institutions such as private property, the courts, and more. There is no basis for the view that markets and governments operate in opposition to each other. See, for example, Rosenberg and Birdzell (1986) for a discussion of the critical role of rules and institutions in Western economic development.

55 Regulations are the means by which governments translate broad social and political goals into manageable tasks to achieve specific outcomes. This is how bureaucracies implement policies by translating the political goals of legislators into manageable tasks for officials. The secret to good regulatory practice thus often lies in appropriate definitions of goals. When goals are poorly defined, regulations become task driven, expensive, and are not well received. For an excellent explanation of the difference between effective and ineffective regulation, see the introduction in James Q. Wilson (1989).

56 A good overview of the extent of convergence and difference can be found in the OECD program on regulatory reform, particularly the country studies on Canada and the United States (see OECD 1999, 2002).

57 For example, the SCC and the US National Institute for Standards Technology (NIST) manage a 1994 agreement for the mutual recognition of the testing laboratory systems they each administer. For the benefit of an industry that exports $1 billion in fasteners annually to the United States, the SCC has concluded an agreement with relevant American agencies so that assessments for conformity with US regulations on Canadian-made fasteners can be performed in Canada.

58 These costs represent 2.7 percent of total 2001 Canada-US trade in goods; specific truck-related costs represent 4.02 percent of total truck-based trade. Transit time and uncertainty costs are estimated at US$4.01 billion and trade-policy-related costs totalled an estimated US$6.28 billion (John C. Taylor and Associates 2003).

59 This, of course, is not a view shared among customs and immigration officials, many of whom hold that no cost is too large to protect the country from illegal drugs, immigrants and other criminal activity. This perspective was well represented by a story planted in Canadian newspapers on 22 July 2003 by the union representing customs officials. See Naumetz (2003).

60 To combat terrorism and other illegal activity, for example, Canada and the United States need rapid and timely exchanges of information on criminals and other individuals who may pose a security risk. Although there is information-sharing at the moment, it may need to be significantly upgraded and some of the information databases need to be combined and made available at the border. Information from law enforcement agencies, immigration agencies, the courts and other institutions may need to be jointly accessible at the

border in real time. There is a need for much greater collaboration and better information management. The database management tools and software developed in the last five years, as well as leading-edge networking software, can be deployed at the border and connected to main databases in Canada and the United States.

61 Canada and the United States already have a wealth of experience to draw on in designing appropriate institutional mechanisms, including the Permanent Joint Board of Defense and the International Joint Commission. One of the lessons that emerges from a study of the operations of these institutions is that their strength is often derived from the quality of their appointments and the insistence of these appointees on maintaining an arm's-length relationship with the government of the day. Committees and task forces of officials, on the other hand, suffer from a lack of independence and are thus easily captured by short-term political and bureaucratic agendas.

62 Leonard Legault, former Canadian co-chair of the International Joint Commission, ascribes the success of the IJC to "its binational but unitary character; its permanence and independence; its impartiality and commitment to solutions that focus on the common interest of both countries; its emphasis on consensus-building; its comprehensive use of joint fact-finding procedures through the establishment of binational advisory boards; and finally, its accessibility to all persons or bodies who wish to put their views before the Commission. Thus, the Commission generally bypasses the disadvantages of government-to-government negotiations and offers certain advantages that go beyond most dispute-settlement mechanisms. As with all institutions, however, the Commission is only as good as its membership. Much depends upon the quality of appointments by the two governments" (2002).

References

Adams, M., with A. Langstaff and D. Jamieson. 2003. *Fire and Ice: The United States, Canada and the Myth of Converging Values*. Toronto: Penguin.

Angell, N. 1910. *The Great Illusion: A Study of the Relation of Military Power in Nations to their Economic and Social Advantage*. London: W. Heinemann.

Axworthy, L. 2003. *Navigating in a New World*. Toronto: Knopf.

Ball, G.W. 1968. *The Discipline of Power: Essentials of a Modern World Structure*. Boston: Little Brown.

Banting, K., G. Hoberg, and R. Simeon, eds. 1997. *Degrees of Freedom: Canada and the United States in a Changing World*. Montreal and Kingston: McGill-Queen's University Press.

Barrett, C.A., and H. Williams. 2003. "Renewing the Relationship: Canada and the United States in the 21st Century." *Inside Edge* 7, no. 2: 7. www.conference-board.ca

Barry, D. 2003. *Managing Canada-US Relations in the post-9/11 Era: Do We Need a Big Idea?* Policy Paper on the Americas, 14, study 11. Washington, DC: Center for Strategic and International Studies.www.csis.org.americas/pubs/pp0311barry.pdf

Boychuk, G., and K. Banting. 2003. "The Paradox of Convergence: National versus Subnational Patterns of Convergence in Canadian and US Income Maintenance Policy." In *North American Linkages: Opportunities and Challenges for Canada*, ed. R. Harris. Calgary: University of Alberta.

Burney, D. 2003. "Twin Pillars of Pragmatism." Address to Canada-US Law Institute annual conference, Case Western Reserve University, Cleveland, Ohio, 11 April.

________. 2004. "The Risk of Complacency, The Need for Engagement." *Policy Options* 25, no. 1: 46-51.

Campbell, B. 2003. *From Deep Integration to Reclaiming Sovereignty: Managing Canada-U.S. Economic Relations under NAFTA*. Ottawa: Canadian Centre for Policy Alternatives. http://www.policyalternatives.ca

Canada. Department of Foreign Affairs and International Trade (DFAIT). 2003. *NAFTA at Ten: A Preliminary Report*. Ottawa: Supply and Services Canada.

________. House of Commons Standing Committee on Foreign Affairs and International Trade. 2002. *Partners in North America: Advancing Canada's Relations with*

the United States and Mexico. http://www.parl.gc.ca/InfoComDoc/ 37/2/FAIT/Studies/Reports/faitr03-e.pdf

_______. Industry Canada. 2002. *North American Regulatory Cooperation*. Ottawa: Supply and Services Canada.

_______. Senate Standing Committee on Foreign Affairs. 2003. *Uncertain Access: The Consequences of U.S. Security and Trade Actions for Canadian Trade Policy*, 1: Report. Ottawa: The Standing Committee.

Centre for Research and Information in Canada (CRIC). 2003."Canadians Differ from Americans on Iraq, United Nations, but Only 1 in 4 Seek More Distant Ties with the US." New release, 9 April. www.cric.ca/en_html/publications2004/ sondages_cric.html

Chambers, E.J., and P.H. Smith, eds. 2002. *NAFTA in the New Millennium*. Calgary: University of Alberta Press.

Clarkson, S. 2002. "Time to Break Free (Trade)." *Globe and Mail*, 27 September.

Conference Board of Canada. 2002. *Performance and Potential 2002-2003*. www.conference-board.ca

Courchene, T., 2003. "FTA at 15, NAFTA at 10: A Canadian Perspective on North American Integration." *North American Journal of Economics and Finance* 14:263-85. This paper was presented at the conference "The Art of the State II: Thinking North America: Prospects and Pathways." Institute for Research on Public Policy, Montebello, Quebec, 16-18 October.

Courchene, T., and R. Harris. 1999. "From Fixing to Monetary Union: Options for North American Currency Integration." *C.D. Howe Institute Commentary* 127. Toronto: C.D. Howe Institute.

Cross, P. 2002. "Cyclical Implications of the Rising Import Content in Exports." *Canadian Economic Observer* (December). http://www.statcan.ca/english/ ads/11-010-XPB/pdf/dec02.pdf

Curtis, J. 2003. "What We Know about Integration So Far." Paper presented at the conference "Art of the State II: Thinking North America: Prospects and Pathways" Institute for Research on Public Policy, Montebello, Quebec, 16-18 October.

Dales, J.H. 1966. *The Protective Tariff in Canada's Development*. Toronto: University of Toronto Press.

de Mestral, A., with Jan Winter. 2003. "A Proposal for a Draft Treaty Giving Direct Effect to NAFTA." Paper presented at the conference "Art of the State II: Thinking North America: Prospects and Pathways" Institute for Research on Public Policy, Montebello, Quebec, 16-18 October.

Dobbin, M. 2003. "Zip Locking North America: Can Canada Survive Continental Integration?" Ottawa: The Council of Canadians. http://www. canadians.org/documents/ ZipLockingNA.pdf

Dobson, W. 2002. "Shaping the Future of North American Economic Space: A Framework for Action." *C.D. Howe Institute Commentary* 162. Toronto: C.D. Howe Institute.

Dodge, D. 2003. "Economic Integration in North America." Remarks at the 72 annual conference, Couchiching Institute on Public Affairs, Orillia, Ontario, 7 August. http://www.banko fcanada.ca/en/speeches/ 2003/sp03-11.htm

Doern, B.G., L.A. Pal, and B.W. Tomlin. 1996. *Border Crossings: The Internationalization of Canadian Public Policy*. Toronto: Oxford University Press.

Dymond, W., and M. Hart. 2001a. *Canadian Cultural Policy, Ownership Restrictions, and Evolving International Trade Rules*. Paper prepared for Heritage Canada (October 2001). On file at the Centre for Trade Policy and Law, Ottawa.

_______. 2001b. *Common Borders, Shared Destinies: Canada, the United States and Deepening Integration*. Ottawa: Centre for Trade Policy and Law.

_______. 2002. "A Canada-EU FTA is an Awful Idea." *Policy Options* 23, no. 5: 27-32.

_______. 2003. "Canada and the Global Challenge: Finding a Place to Stand." *C.D. Howe Institute Commentary* 180. Toronto: C.D. Howe Institute.

_______. 2004. "The Potemkin Village of Canadian Foreign Policy." *Policy Options* 25, no. 1: 39-45.

Ekos Research Associates. 2000. "Canadian Public Opinion: International Trade Issues 1999." 20 May.

Elliott, K.A., J.J. Schott, G.C. Hufbauer, and B. Oegg. 2004. *Economic Sanctions Reconsidered*. Washington, DC: Institute for International Economies.

Fagan, D. 2002. "This Problem Borders on Urgent." *Globe and Mail*, 11 December, A13.

________. 2003. "How to Stay the Slippery Slide of Canada-US Relations." *Globe and Mail*, 1 April.

Fry, E. 2003. *North American Economic Integration: Policy Options*. Policy Paper on the Americas 14, study 8. Washington, DC: Center for Strategic and International Studies. http://www.csis.org/amecas/pubs/pp_Namerican EconomicIntegration (July%202003).pdf

Galbraith, J.K. 1985. "Canadian Customs." *Saturday Night*, January.

Globerman, S. 2003. "Assessing Recent Patterns of Foreign Direct Investment in Canada and the United States." In *North American Linkages: Opportunities and Challenges for Canada*, ed. R. Harris. Calgary: University of Calgary Press.

Goldfarb, D. 2003. "Beyond Labels: Comparing Proposals for Closer Canada-US Economic Relations." *Backgrounder* 76. Toronto: C.D. Howe Institute.

________. 2003. "The Road to a Canada-US Customs Union: Step-by-Step or in a Single Bound?" *C.D. Howe Institute Commentary* 184. Toronto: C.D. Howe Institute.

Gotlieb, A. 1991. *"I Will Be with you in a minute, Mr. Ambassador..." The Education of a Canadian Diplomat in Washington*. Toronto: University of Toronto Press.

________. 2002a. "Getting Attention." *National Post*, 17 May. www.nationalpost.com

________. 2002b."Why Not a Grand Bargain with the US." *National Post,* 11 September.

________. 2003a. "Canada Must Return to its 'Golden Age' of Diplomacy." *National Post*, 10 September, A16.

________. 2003b. "A Grand Bargain with the US." *National Post*, 5 March.

________. 2003c. "A North American Community of Law." Paper presented at a conference at the Woodrow Wilson Center in Washington, 27 February.

________. 2003d. "Troubling Vision of a Dark Force." *National Post*," 15 November.

Graham, W. 2003. "Sovereignty, Independence, and Integration." Paper presented at the 72nd annual conference, Couchiching Institute on Public Affairs, Orillia, Ontario, 7-10 August. http://webapps.dfait-maeci.gc.ca/minpub/ Publication.asp?

Granatstein, J. 2003. "The Importance of Being Less Earnest: Promoting Canada's National Interests through Tighter Ties with the US." C.D. Howe Benefactors Lecture. www.cdhowe.org

Greenspon, E. 2001. "Building the New Canadian." *Globe and Mail*, 10 November.

Greenspon, E., and D. Bricker. 2001. *Searching for Certainty: Inside the New Canadian Mindset*. Toronto: Doubleday.

Hakim, P., and R.E. Litan, eds. 2002. *The Future of North American Integration: Beyond NAFTA*. Washington, DC: The Brookings Institution.

Harris, R., ed. 2003. *North American Linkages: Opportunities and Challenges for Canada*. Calgary: University of Calgary Press.

Harris. R., and N. Schmitt. 2003. "The Consequences of Increased Labour Mobility within an Integrating North America." In *North American Linkages: Opportunities and Challenges for Canada*, ed. R. Harris. Calgary: University of Calgary Press.

Hart, M. 1996. *Doing the Right Thing: Regional Integration and the Multilateral Trade Regime*, Occasional Paper no. 39. Ottawa: Centre for Trade Policy and Law.

________. 2002. *A Trading Nation: Canadian Trade Policy from Colonialism to Globalization*. Vancouver: University of British Columbia Press.

________. 2002/03. "Lessons from Canada's History as a Trading Nation." *International Journal* 58, no. 1: 25-42.

Hart. M., ed. 2000. "Canada-US Free Trade: Is It Time for Round Two — A Virtual Roundtable." *Canadian Foreign Policy* 7 (spring): 3.

Helliwell, J. 1998. *How Much Do National Borders Matter?* Washington, DC: The Brookings Institution.

________. 2002. *Globalization and Well-Being*. Vancouver: University of British Columbia Press.

Henderson, D. 1994. "Putting 'Trade Blocs' into Perspective." In *Trade Blocs? The Future of Regional Integration*, ed. V. Cable and D.

Henderson. London: Royal Institute of International Affairs.

Hufbauer, G., and J.G. Schott. 2004. "The Prospects for Deeper North American Economic Integration: An American Perspective Post-9/11." *C.D. Howe Institute Commentary* 195. Toronto: C.D. Howe Institute.

Ipsos-Reid. 2003. "Canadians and Americans Reflect on Cross-Border Business in a Post9/11 World." www.ipsos-reid.com/ media/dsp_displaypr_cdn.cfm?id_to_view=1939

Jackson, A. 2003. *Why the 'Big Idea' is a Bad Idea: A Critical Perspective on Deeper Economic Integration with the United States*. Ottawa: Canadian Centre for Policy Alternatives.

Janigan, M. 2003. "A Room of One's Own," *Maclean's*, 24 November. www.macleans.ca/ swit...article.jsp?content=20031124_70130_70130

John C. Taylor and Associates. 2003. "The US-Canada Border: Border Economic Costs, Their Causes, and Alternative Border Management Strategies." Seidman School of Business, Grand Valley State University, Michigan

Kreinin, M.E., ed. 2000. *Building a Partnership: The Canada-United States Free Trade Agreement*. East Lansing, MI: Michigan State University Press.

Legault, L. 2002. "Canada and the United States: Three Ways to Run a Relationship." Remarks to the Ottawa Chapter of the Canadian Institute of International Affairs, Ottawa, 7 November.

Lipset, S.M. 1989. *Continental Divide: The Values and Institutions of the United States and Canada*. Toronto and Washington: C.D. Howe Institute and the Canadian-American Committee.

MacDonald, L.I., ed. 2000. *Free Trade: Risks and Rewards*. Montreal and Kingston: McGill-Queen's University Press.

Mackenzie King Papers, Public Archives of Canada. 1968. Reproduced in *Canadian Foreign Policy: Historical Readings*, ed. J.L. Granatstein. Toronto: Copp Clark Pitman.

Macrory, P. 2002. "Dispute Settlement in the NAFTA: A Surprising Record of Success." *C.D. Howe Institute Commentary* 168. Toronto: C.D. Howe Institute.

McCallum, J., and J. Helliwell. 1994. "National Borders Still Matter for Trade." *Policy Options* 15 (July/August): 44-48.

McCarthy, S. 2003a. "Canadians Vote Bush Least-Liked President." *Globe and Mail*, 12 July. www.theglobeandmail.com/ servlet/story/RTGAM.20030712.upoll0712/BNStory/National

________. 2003b. "Large Majority Backs Free Trade." *Globe and Mail*, 9 June. www.theglobeandmail.com/servlet/ArticleNews/TPPrint/LAC/2003060/UPOLLN2/TPNational

McDougall, J. 2003. "The Long-Run Determinants of Deep/Political Canada-US Integration." Paper presented at the conference, "Art of the State II: Thinking North America: Prospects and Pathways." Institute for Research on Public Policy, Montebello, Quebec, 17-18 October.

McKinney, J.A. 2003. "Deeper United States-Canada Economic Integration: Is It Desirable? Is It Inevitable?" Paper prepared for presentation at the Southern Canadian Studies Association conference, Atlanta, 15-16 August.

Mendelsohn, M., and R. Wolfe. 2000. "Probing the Aftermyth of Seattle: Canada Public Opinion on International Trade 1980-2000." Paper prepared for the National Policy Research Conference, Ottawa, 1 December.

Mirus, R. 2001. "After Sept 11: A Canada-US Customs Union." *Policy Options* 22, no. 9: 50-52.

Monnet, J. 1978. *Memoirs*. Garden City, NJ: Doubleday.

Mulroney, Brian. 2002. Remarks made at "NAFTA at Ten Conference," Woodrow Wilson Center, Washington, December.

Naumetz, T. 2003. "Summer Border Policy: Take Operational Risks." *National Post*, 22 July, A2.

Newman, P. 2003. "Beware of Freer Trade." *Maclean's*, 2 December.

Olewiler, N. 2003. "North American Integration and the Environment." In *North American Linkages: Opportunities and Challenges for Canada*, ed. R. Harris. Calgary: University of Calgary Press.

Organisation for Economc Co-operation and Development (OECD). 1999. *Government Capacity to Assure High Quality Regulation*. Paris: OECD. http://www.oecd.org/dataoecd/ 48/19/2478900.pdf

________. 2002. Canada: *Maintaining Leadership through Innovation*. Paris: OECD.

http://www1.oecd.org/publications/e-book/4202091E.PDF

Ostry, S., and G. Winham. 2003. "The Second Trade Crisis." *Globe and Mail*, 17 June.

Pastor, R. 2001. *Toward a North American Community: Lessons from the Old World for the New*. Washington, DC: Institute for International Economics.

Pettigrew, P. 2002. "The Canada We Want in the North America We Are Building." Address to the 8th annual Canadian-American Business Achievement Award and International Business Partnership Forum, Toronto, 16 October. http://webapps.dfaitmaeci.gc.ca/minpub/ Publication.asp

________. 2003a. "Canada, US and Mexico Reject Customs Union as Next Step." *National Post*, 8 October, B19.

________. 2003b. "Dancing with the Elephant: Contending with an Assertive Superpower in Trade and Global Diplomacy." Speech at the Empire Club, 25 September. http://webapps.dfait-maeci.gc.ca/ minpub/ Publication.asp?

Pettigrew, Pierre S., Fernando Canales, and Robert B. Zoellick. 2003. "Celebrating NAFTA at Ten." NAFTA Free Trade Commission Joint Statement. Department of Foreign Affairs and Internal Trade Canada. www.dfait-maeci.gc.ca/nafta-alena/statement-en.asp

Rekai, P. 2002. "US and Canadian Immigration Policies: Marching Together to Different Tunes." *C.D. Howe Institute Commentary* 171. Toronto: C.D. Howe Institute.

Rosenberg, N., and L.E. Birdzell. 1986. *How the West Grew Rich: The Economic Transformation of the Industrialized World*. New York: Basic Books.

Schwanen, D. 2001. "Interoperability with the US, not Convergence." *Policy Options* 22, no. 9: 46-49.

________. 2003. "Let's Not Cut Corners: Unbundling the Canada-US Relationship." *Policy Options* 24, no. 4: 12-19.

Scotton, G. 2002. "Panel Urges Continental Customs Union Plan." *Calgary Herald*, 27 September.

Sears, R. 2002. "With Sovereignty, Less is More." *Toronto Star*, 4 May, H1.

Segal, H. 2002. "New North American Institutions: The Need for Creative Statecraft." Address to the Fifth Annual JLT/CTPL Trade Law Conference, Ottawa, 18 April. http://www.irpp.org/ fasttrak/ index.htm

St. Jacques, R. 2003. "Sovereignty or Standard of Living: Is There a Trade-Off?" Paper presented at the 72nd annual conference, Couchiching Institute on Public Affairs, Orillia, Ontario, 7-10 August. www.couch.ca/history/index.html

Stairs, D. 2001. "Canada in the 1990s: Speak Loudly and Carry a Bent Twig." *Policy Options* 22, no. 1: 43-50.

________. 2003. "Myths, Morals, and Reality in Canadian Foreign Policy." *International Journal* 58, no. 1: 2.

Tomlin, B., and B. Doern. 1991. *Faith and Fear: The Free Trade Story*. Toronto: Stoddart.

Watson, W. 1998. *Globalization and the Meaning of Canadian Life*. Toronto: University of Toronto Press.

Weber, T. 2003. "Canadians Seek Closer Ties with US, Poll Says." *Globe and Mail*, 25 March. www.pollara.ca.new/Library/ surveys/supporortfcloserties.htm

Weintraub, S. 1994. *NAFTA: What Comes Next?* Washington, DC: Center for Strategic and International Studies.

Welch, Jennifer. 2003. "Prospects and Pathways for North American Integration: The Implications for Citizenship." Paper presented at the conference "The Art of the State II: Thinking North America: Prospects and Pathways." Institute for Research on Public Policy, Montebello, Quebec, 16-18 October.

Wilson, J.Q. 1989. *Bureaucracy: What Government Agencies Do and Why They Do It*. New York: Basic Books.

Wistrich, E. 1991. *After 1992: The United States of Europe*. London: Routledge.

Wolfe, R. 2003. "See You in Washington? A Pluralist Perspective on North American Institutions." IRPP *Choices* 9, no. 4. Montreal: Institute for Research on Public Policy.

Yussuf, Hassan. 2003. "Sovereignty or Standard of Living." Notes for a speech presented at the 72nd Annual Conference, Couchiching Institute on Public Affairs, Orillia, Ontario, 7-10 August. www.couch.ca

Michael Hart is Simon Reisman Professor of Trade Policy at the Norman Paterson School of International Affairs at Carleton University and a Distinguished Fellow at the Centre for Trade Policy and Law at Carleton University. He was an official in Canada's Department of Foreign Affairs and International Trade.